BRAND
STRATEGY

Lay the Foundation for
a Purpose-Driven Business

Branding Essentials For Small Business

A Practical Workbook Series to
Build a Brand with Clarity, Confidence, and Purpose

The book you're holding right now!

BOOK 1:
Brand Strategy – Lay the Foundation for a Purpose-Driven Business
Before you design a logo or write a tagline, you need clarity on what your brand stands for. This book helps you define your purpose, values, audience, and brand direction so every decision you make is rooted in strategy.

BOOK 2:
Brand Personality – Create Meaningful Connection Through Identity, Voice, and Messaging
Your business already has a personality, whether you've defined it or not. This book helps you shape your brand's character traits, emotional fingerprint, voice, tone, and style.

BOOK 3:
Brand Positioning – Own Your Niche and Be Remembered
Clarify your unique place in the market so the right people remember and choose you. This book walks you through strategically positioning your brand and standing out without shouting.

BOOK 4:
Brand Audit – From Confusion to Clarity for Strategic Growth
If your brand feels inconsistent or outdated, this guide will help you assess what's working, what's not, and how to refresh your brand without starting from scratch.

Download the Exercises

Download a printable version of all the exercises at TrembleDesign.com/BrandBooks **(or scan the QR code below)**. This free companion resource also gives you access to additional tools and invites you to join my email list for ongoing support and announcements about future book releases in the series.

BRAND

Strategy

Lay the Foundation for
a Purpose-Driven Business

Pam Tremble

BOOK 1 | BRANDING ESSENTIALS FOR SMALL BUSINESS

ORDERING INFORMATION:

Quantity sales. Special discounts are available on quantity purchases by corporations, associations, and others. Book signings and appearances can be arranged by contacting the author at Pam@TrembleDesign.com.

Published by Tremble Creative Services, LLC | DBA Tremble Design Studio

Printed in the United States of America.

Brand Strategy: Lay the Foundation for a Purpose-Driven Business

Book 1 | *Brand Building for Small Business series*

ISBN: 978-0-9888310-4-9

Contact the author

3193 Boardwalk Drive #5132 • Saginaw, MI 48603
pam@trembledesign.com | TrembleDesign.com/BrandBooks

CONTENTS

Preface 1

Introduction 4

PART 1: Brand Foundations 10

CHAPTER 1: What Is a Brand, Really?. 12

Exercise: Define Your Brand in Your Own Words 18

CHAPTER 2: Brand Purpose 22

Exercise: Clarify Your Purpose 30

CHAPTER 3: Brand Values 36

Exercise: Core Values Discovery 43

CHAPTER 4: Brand Personality 48

Exercise: Define Your Brand Voice 56

CHAPTER 5: Your Audience 60

Exercise: Define Your Right-Fit Audience. 68

CHAPTER 6: Brand Positioning 74

Exercise: Write Your Positioning Statement 81

PART 2: From Strategy to Action 88

CHAPTER 7: Bringing It All Together 90

Exercise: Brand Strategy Summary Sheet 95

CHAPTER 8: Audit, Evolve, and Grow. 102

Continue Your Branding Journey 112

APPENDIX: Glossary of Brand Terms. 114

PREFACE

My Branding Story
The Long Road to Intention

My design career started long before I launched my business. I worked for years as a senior graphic designer and later as a creative director – all while running a freelance side hustle on nights and weekends.

When I left full-time employment, I leaned into that foundation and built my own design studio, specializing in building brand systems for small businesses, solopreneurs, consultants, and nonprofits. But I didn't start with a goal of growing big or fast. In fact, I'd already had a brief stint as the co-founder of a traditional design agency, and I quickly realized that model wasn't a good fit for me.

I'm at my best when I have creative control and the space to work independently. I've intentionally chosen to stay solo, not out of fear of growth, but because I value autonomy and flexibility. When I do grow my business, it's through deliberate choices that support my lifestyle and align with the values that feed my entrepreneurial soul.

As I stepped into full-time entrepreneurship, I rediscovered who I was and what I wanted my business to become. I asked myself hard questions about what I wanted my business to be and how life would be different after climbing the corporate ladder for more than two decades.

The answers all pointed back to my core values and my purpose. If I were to build something of my own, it would need to reflect what I believed in. Not just my personal values, but laying a foundation for the values that my business stands on and the purpose behind my work for clients.

That's the foundation I help other business owners uncover through my comprehensive process of building an effective brand strategy. And that's the process I'll take you through in this book.

A Company of One (by choice)

After a 22-year career in design and creative direction, I built something different – a business centered on freedom, flexibility, and meaningful client relationships. I no longer manage departments or climb corporate ladders. Instead, I pour my creative energy into client work I care about and leave space for travel, art, and the quiet joys of solo work.

I'm a company of one by design. Sometimes, I collaborate with other professionals on projects, but at the end of the day, I return to my solo business where I do my best work.

If you're not a solo business owner, don't let that stop you. This workbook is for anyone making brand decisions – whether you lead a team of hundreds or just you and your cat. Regardless of the size of your business, an intentional brand strategy is essential for long-term success.

The DIY-First Philosophy

I've always been a curious learner – okay, maybe a bit of a nerd. I enjoy understanding how things work. I read books, attend workshops, talk to experts, and tap into business resources like the SBA and local business development centers. Jumping down random rabbit holes is my favorite pastime!

I love the DIY-first approach to business because I love having my hands in everything. But that doesn't mean I will do everything myself forever. I hire professionals when I need to. But it's essential to make informed decisions before bringing in pros to help me.

For example, I don't need to be a CPA to manage my daily business finances. Still, I worked hard to understand bookkeeping basics and how certain business decisions affect my financial picture. It's about gaining enough understanding so I can confidently evaluate my options and ask the right questions when it's time to bring in a professional when I'm ready.

Having that foundational understanding of my business finances helps me know exactly what I need and how to assess whether a professional is the right fit for my business.

That's the heart of the DIY-first mindset. It's not about doing everything yourself forever or being frugal or scrappy – it's about being intentional, informed, and in control of your business.

Yes, there's a risk of getting stuck in research mode. I've been there. But the more you understand your brand, the easier it is to lead with clarity – and communicate that clarity to future collaborators and customers. This book is one step in helping you get there.

Before You Begin

You don't need to be a designer, a strategist, or a branding expert to build a strong brand. You just need a willingness to think deeply, reflect honestly, and take one intentional step at a time.

If this process feels overwhelming at first, that's okay. It's normal to have questions. You might not have all the answers right away, but by slowing down and spending time with each chapter, you'll build clarity and confidence as you go.

The point isn't to create a perfect brand strategy on your first try. The point is to create a solid foundation you can grow with. And if that foundation reflects your purpose, values, and speaks to your audience, you'll be ahead of most businesses.

This workbook is here to help you do that. You don't have to do it all at once. Just keep moving forward, one thoughtful step at a time.

INTRODUCTION

This is both an instructional book and an action-oriented workbook. If you simply read the words on these pages, you'll walk away with a solid understanding of what brand strategy is and why it matters to your business. But if you take the time to complete the exercises and worksheets at the end of each chapter, you'll walk away with something even more valuable: a brand strategy that's uniquely yours.

There's a lot of noise in the business world about "building a brand." But you need a strong foundation before investing in visuals or marketing tactics. This workbook is here to help you create that brand foundation. That foundation isn't about trendy logos or social media hacks; it's about defining the deeper strategy that guides every decision you make – and ensuring that your brand reflects who you are and how you serve.

Who This Workbook Is For

This workbook is for small business owners of all kinds – solopreneurs, small teams, nonprofit leaders, coaches, and consultants – who want to build a brand that reflects their values, personality, business goals, and way of working.

Even though I run a solo business myself, this book isn't just for solopreneurs. Whether you're a team of one or the leader of a small organization, every brand decision starts with you. You're the one setting the tone, communicating the values, and defining what success looks like.

Maybe you're just starting and unsure where to begin. Maybe you're knee-deep in business planning and need guidance for your brand strategy. Or maybe you've been in business for a while, and your current brand no longer fits, holding you back from reaching the next growth phase.

Wherever you are in your journey, this book will walk you through a DIY-first approach to creating a thoughtful, values-based brand strategy, one that aligns your messaging, visuals, offers, and customer experience. Branding is more than a logo; it's your internal compass for how your business shows up in the world.

What Is Brand Strategy and Why Does It Come First

A brand is more than a logo, a tagline, or a beautifully designed website. It's the heartbeat of your business. It's how your audience experiences, connects with, and ultimately trusts what you offer.

Like any strong business, you need a plan to ensure that every part of your brand works together clearly and consistently. Brand strategy is that plan. It defines your purpose, values, voice, audience, and positioning. It lays the groundwork for how your business is perceived and understood long before you even open graphic design software, write your website copy, or launch a marketing campaign.

Without a clear strategy, branding becomes disjointed and reactive. You may find yourself constantly changing your messaging, experimenting with design styles that don't stick, or attracting the wrong audience.

It becomes harder to build recognition, trust, or momentum. But when your brand strategy is solid, everything else – your visuals, marketing, offers, and communications – has something to align with. You gain direction. You build confidence. You start to sound like you.

A strong brand strategy empowers you to:

- Attract the right audience and build meaningful connections

- Define a personality that feels like an extension of who you are as a business owner

- Craft clear, compelling messaging that communicates your values, purpose, and mission

- Stand out in your industry with unique positioning

Your brand is more human than you might realize. It has character, tone, and personality. That's why you can't create meaningful design or marketing materials if you haven't first defined the heart of your brand.

When your strategy is clear, decisions become easier, marketing becomes more effective, messaging resonates, offers connect, and your brand feels cohesive, because it actually is.

This workbook starts here: not with visuals or promotion, but with the foundational strategy that makes every other piece stronger, smarter, and more aligned.

What This Book Covers and How It Fits Into the Bigger Picture

This workbook is focused entirely on brand strategy, the foundation of how your business shows up in the world. Inside, you'll define your core values, purpose, vision, voice, audience, and brand positioning. These elements form the strategic backbone of your brand and influence everything else you create, from visuals to marketing to customer experience.

While brand strategy and business strategy often overlap, this book won't dive into the operational or financial side of running a business. We also won't be building out a full marketing plan here. Instead, you'll focus on the internal clarity that allows your marketing and messaging to be more effective later on.

Think of this workbook as the prep work before design, marketing, or promotion. It's here to help you build a brand that's aligned from the inside out, so when you create visuals, write content, or launch offers, they'll actually feel like you.

This Book Is Part of a Series

This is the first book in the **Brand Building for Small Business** series, a collection of short, practical workbooks designed to help solopreneurs and small business owners confidently create a values-aligned brand.

Each book in the series focuses on one essential element of brand building, from strategy and voice to visuals, positioning, and beyond. Together, they guide you through the full process of creating a cohesive, authentic brand that reflects who you are and resonates with the people you're built to serve.

Whether you're just starting out or refining an existing identity, this four-book series gives you the tools and clarity to build a clear, consistent, and impactful brand.

Book 1: Brand Strategy
Lay the foundation for a purpose-driven business

Book 2: Brand Personality
Create meaningful connection through identity, voice, and messaging

Book 3: Brand Positioning
Own your niche and be remembered

Book 4: Brand Audit
From confusion to clarity for strategic growth

You can read these books individually to solve a specific need, or work through them as a complete system for building or refreshing your brand over time. Either way, the goal is the same: to give you clear, approachable tools to help you build a brand that reflects your business and values.

How to Use This Workbook

This is a hands-on workbook designed to help you understand the foundational elements of your brand strategy. Each chapter includes two main parts: straightforward, conversational guidance to help you understand the concept and a workbook-style exercise to help you apply the idea to your business in a practical way.

At the back of the book, you'll also find a glossary of brand terms. If you come across a term that's new to you, or you just want to clarify the difference between brand and branding, it's all there. This reference is meant to support your learning without overwhelming you with jargon.

Take your time, reflecting as you go. You don't need to complete everything in one sitting—this is your process.

Download the Exercises

Download a printable version of all the exercises at TrembleDesign.com/BrandBooks **(or scan the QR code below)**. This free companion resource also gives you access to additional tools and invites you to join my email list for ongoing support and announcements about future book releases in the series.

PART 1
BRAND FOUNDATIONS

Before designing a logo, writing your About page, or sharing your message with the world, you must know what your brand stands for. This first section is all about defining the foundation on which everything else will be built.

You'll clarify your purpose, values, voice, audience, and positioning, the core components shaping how your business shows up and how people connect with your offer.

This isn't just strategy for strategy's sake. It's practical, human-centered brand work that will help you make decisions faster, communicate more clearly, and build a business that feels like you from the inside out.

You don't need to get everything perfect before you move forward. But the more clarity you create here, the easier it becomes to grow with intention, consistency, and confidence.

CHAPTER 1
What Is a Brand, Really?

Let's start with something simple, but surprisingly misunderstood (and often debated): **What is a brand?**

Most people jump straight to logos, fonts, or color palettes when they hear the word "branding." And yes, those are part of it – but they're not the whole story. Not even close. Your brand isn't your logo. It's not your Instagram feed, your business cards, or the design of your website.

Your brand is your reputation. It's what people think, feel, and say about your business when you're not in the room. It's the impression you leave behind. It's the experience people have when they interact with your services, your messaging, your client process, or your team.

Your brand is how your business makes people feel.

That might sound soft or vague at first, but it has real weight. The perception you create influences who chooses to work with you, how much they trust you, what they expect from you, and whether they'll come back or refer others.

Let's look at a few familiar examples:

- **Johnson & Johnson** baby products evoke feelings of gentleness, safety, and deep care. Everything about the brand—from the soft color palette to the messaging— communicates comfort and trust. It's not just about shampoo; it's about protecting what's most precious.

- **Nike**, on the other hand, taps into energy, motivation, and competition. The brand makes you feel like an athlete–even if you're just lacing up for a morning walk. It's aspirational, confident, and focused on achievement through hard work.

- **Airbnb** doesn't just offer vacation rentals. It invites you to belong anywhere. Its brand emphasizes emotional experiences – connection, community, discovery, and home – no matter where you are in the world.

- **Fidelity Investments** is a brand built on trust, consistency, and long-term reliability. It doesn't try to dazzle with flash – it aims to reassure. The brand communicates stability, expertise, and a steady hand, which people want when considering their retirement, investments, or financial future.

These brands all have one thing in common: they've created a consistent emotional experience to connect with their audience on a more human level. That emotional experience is what makes people remember them and choose them again and again.

As a small business owner, you don't need to be Nike or Fidelity. But you need to be clear on what experience you want your audience to have – and how you'll consistently deliver it.

That clarity is where brand strategy begins.

Branding vs. Marketing: What's the Difference?

People often use "branding" and "marketing" interchangeably, but they're different. Confusing the two can lead to wasted time, money, and energy. While they're closely connected, each serves a distinct purpose in your business.

Here's a simple breakdown:

- **Your brand is who you are.** It's the soul of your business; the values you believe in, the people you serve, the personality you express, and the promise you make to your customers.

- **Your branding is how you express who you are.** It shows up in your voice, visuals, client experience, and internal culture. It's how your business looks, sounds, and feels across every touchpoint.

- **Your marketing is how you share who you are with others.**
  It includes the tools, platforms, and strategies you use to attract the right people and encourage them to take action.

You can also think of it like this:

- **Branding** happens behind the scenes. It's strategic, foundational, and internal.

- **Marketing** happens out in the world. It's visible, fast-moving, and focused on getting attention and results.

Branding gives your marketing meaning. Marketing gives your branding reach.

An analogy that might help: Imagine your business is a house. Brand strategy is the blueprint, it defines the structure, purpose, and function of branding, which is the interior design – the colors on the walls, the lighting, furniture style, and how it feels when someone walks through the door.

Marketing is the invitation to come over – the open house sign, the photos you post online, and the message that says, "This is the place you've been looking for."

If the blueprint is missing or the rooms are poorly designed, no amount of advertising will make people feel at home. The house might look good from the outside, but the experience won't live up to the promise.

That's why brand strategy must come first. It informs everything: your values, visual identity, personality, voice, messaging, your positioning, and even what services or products you offer. When those pieces are solid and aligned, marketing becomes easier and more effective because you're promoting something with clarity and purpose.

When branding is unclear, marketing feels scattered and stressful. But when your brand strategy is strong, marketing becomes an extension of who you are, not a performance you must maintain.

Brand vs. Other Business Terms

Let's clear up a few common terms so you feel grounded going forward. Understanding the difference will help you make better decisions and communicate more clearly when working with others.

- **Brand**: Your business's identity, personality, and reputation

- **Brand Strategy**: The internal foundation that defines your purpose, values, audience, voice, and position

- **Branding**: The practice of creating the look, feel, tone, and experience of your brand

- **Brand Identity**: The logo, colors, fonts, imagery, and other visual elements

- **Marketing**: The methods you use to reach and attract your ideal audience

- **Content**: The material you produce to share your message (social posts, blogs, newsletters, etc.)

You don't need to become an expert in all of these, but knowing the distinctions will help you speak your business's language with more confidence, especially when working with designers, strategists, or marketing professionals.

Want more definitions?
Check out the full glossary of brand strategy terms at the back of this book. Use it as a quick reference guide as you work through this book.

Why This Matters for You

If you're building a business that reflects your values and goals, your brand should also reflect that. Whether you're a solo consultant, a creative service provider, or the director of a small nonprofit, the way your business shows up in the world matters.

Your brand shapes the experience your audience has with you long before they sign a contract, make a purchase, or donate to your cause. When it's rooted in a thoughtful strategy, your brand becomes one of the most powerful tools you have.

A clear, values-aligned brand helps people:

- Understand what you do and how you can help them

- Feel confident in your professionalism and reliability

- Decide if you're the right fit for their needs, style, or philosophy

- Form a connection that goes beyond the transactional

But your brand isn't just for your audience, it's for you, too. A clear brand strategy gives you something powerful: direction. It becomes your internal compass, helping you make thoughtful, confident decisions without second-guessing every move.

When you know what your brand stands for, how it communicates, and who it's here to serve, it's easier to stay focused on what really matters, even when there are a dozen different directions you could go.

It also brings a sense of calm and consistency to your brand. Whether you're writing an email, creating a new offer, or pursuing a business opportunity, your strategy reminds you of your values, voice, and vision. It gives you a framework to choose aligned collaborators, refine your message, and say "yes" to the right things, and just as importantly, "no" to the things that don't fit.

When your brand feels like a true reflection of who you are and how you serve, it's not just easier to run your business, and it's more fulfilling, too.

That's why we're starting with strategy. Before we discuss messaging, logos, positioning, or marketing strategy, we'll build your brand's inner structure. We'll begin with your purpose, your audience, and your values because that's where all strong brands start.

This book will guide you through that foundation step-by-step. If you take the time to reflect, write, and clarify as you go, you'll walk away with more than inspiration, you'll have a usable brand strategy that supports your goals and feels true to you.

Strong brands aren't built by accident. They're built with intention. And it all starts right here.

EXERCISE
Define Your Brand in Your Own Words

Before we move on, take a few minutes to write down your thoughts. There are no right or wrong answers here–this is just a starting point. You'll revisit these reflections later in the workbook to see how your thinking has evolved.

Download this Exercise at TrembleDesign.com/BrandBooks
Use the space provided below to answer the questions, or grab the printable version of the exercise pages for additional flexibility.

What does "brand" mean to you?
Don't worry about being correct – just write what comes to mind.

_____

_____

_____

_____

_____

_____

_____

_____

_____

_____

What do you want your brand to feel like to others?
Examples: trustworthy, warm, efficient, joyful, bold, calm

_____

_____

_____

_____

_____

_____

_____

Think of a business you admire. What do you believe their brand is built on? *What impression do they give? What do they seem to stand for?*

_____

_____

_____

_____

_____

_____

_____

Now think of a competitor in your industry, or a business in your space you want to learn from. *What emotions or impressions do you associate with their brand? Do you view them as friendly? Intimidating? Polished? Outdated? What does their brand make you feel – and why?*

_____

_____

_____

_____

_____

_____

_____

_____

_____

_____

_____

_____

_____

_____

CHAPTER 2
Brand Purpose

"He who has a why can endure any how."
– Friedrich Nietzsche

Let's begin with one of the most important pieces of your brand strategy: your purpose or why you do what you do.

Your **brand purpose** is the deeper reason your business exists beyond just making money. The beliefs, motivation, or mission drive your work and connect it to something bigger than the day-to-day tasks.

Your purpose might show up in how you serve your clients, the problem you're passionate about solving, or the future you're trying to help create. It's not about sounding impressive, it's about being true to what matters most to you.

You might have heard this described as your "why." That's exactly what this section is about: defining what drives you to do what you do.

Why Your Why Matters

Knowing your purpose isn't just a feel-good exercise – it gives your business direction and staying power. When you're clear on your why, everything else becomes easier. You'll have a compass to guide decisions, stay grounded through tough seasons, and connect with people more meaningfully.

People start businesses for creative freedom, flexible schedules, and financial independence. But underneath those surface-level goals is often something deeper, a desire for freedom, service, or meaning.

That freedom can look like the ability to solve problems in your own way, the space to build something aligned with your values, and the flexibility to design your work around your life.

But freedom alone isn't enough to sustain a brand. Your purpose is what transforms your business from a list of to-dos into something that matters. It turns your brand into something people connect with and want to support because it feels like it stands for something.

And when business gets hard, messy, or uncertain, your purpose will help you remember why you started in the first place.

Clarifying Your Brand Purpose

Most people live their lives focused on what they have to do—emails, client work, content creation, outreach. But when you lose touch with why you're doing it all, it's easy to feel like you're sprinting on a treadmill that never stops.

When your deeper purpose fades into the background, you risk burnout, exhaustion, and growing your business in a direction that no longer fits. Without a clear why, even success can feel empty or misaligned.

Your brand purpose invites you to step off the treadmill and look around. It helps you zoom out from the daily grind and reconnect with the heart of your business.

Getting clear on your purpose isn't just about crafting the perfect mission statement. It's about being honest with yourself and understanding the kind of brand you genuinely want to build. Ask yourself:

- What change do you want to create?
- Who are you here to serve?
- What lights you up about the work you do?

How Brand Purpose Shapes Your Business

Once you define your purpose, it begins to influence everything else in your business. It becomes a filter through which you can evaluate opportunities, refine your messaging, and shape the experience your audience has with your brand.

Brand purpose isn't just a nice-to-have; it's the backbone of your business decisions. Purpose-driven businesses are more aligned and tend to

- **Attract more aligned clients or customers:** When your purpose is clear, you naturally attract people who resonate with what you stand for.

- **Create stronger, more consistent messaging:** Everything you communicate through your website, social media, or one-on-one interactions becomes more focused and on-brand.

- **Feel more rewarding and sustainable for the founder:** Working towards something you believe in gives you the energy to push through tough times and continue building something meaningful.

Without purpose, your brand may drift. You might find yourself chasing trends, saying yes to clients who aren't a good fit, or creating offers that feel disconnected from what you actually want to deliver.

But with purpose, every decision becomes easier. You know what you stand for and what you don't.

Think of it like a compass. Your purpose keeps you moving in the right direction, even when the path gets tough or the market shifts. It's your constant touchstone for decision-making, ensuring your brand stays true to its core even as you adapt and evolve.

Example: Bookkeeping for Creatives

Let's say you run a bookkeeping service for solopreneurs. Without a clearly defined purpose, you might struggle to stand out. After all, dozens of bookkeepers offer similar services, and the industry can seem crowded.

But if your purpose is "to make money management feel simple and empowering for overwhelmed creatives," suddenly, your message becomes more precise and emotionally relevant to the people you're trying to reach. You're not just offering a service, you're helping creatives focus on what they do best without worrying about the complexities of numbers.

Example: IT and Cybersecurity Consulting

Now, imagine you run a small IT and cybersecurity consultancy. A generic purpose might be "to protect businesses from digital threats," but a stronger, more focused purpose could be:

"To help small businesses feel confident and in control of their technology by making cybersecurity accessible, understandable, and stress-free."

With that clarity, your messaging becomes less about fear and technical jargon and more about empowering your audience. You're positioning yourself as a trusted partner who supports their success, not just a fixer when something goes wrong. This purpose-driven branding builds trust and helps you stand out in an industry often perceived as cold or overly complex.

Example: Wellness Coaching

Consider a wellness coach whose mission is to help people live healthier, more balanced lives. A broad purpose like "helping people get fit" is fine, but a deeper purpose, such as "empowering busy professionals to reclaim their health through sustainable, manageable wellness routines," connects with a specific audience.

This clarity defines who the coach helps and allows the business to tailor services that speak directly to the target audience's pain points, like time management and stress reduction. It also sets the foundation for stronger, more relatable messaging that speaks directly to their audience's challenges.

The Connection Between Personal and Brand Purpose

If you're a solopreneur or small business owner, your personal identity often overlaps with your brand, and that's a good thing. It means your business can feel genuine, grounded, and personal in a way that larger organizations sometimes struggle to achieve.

However, it's also important to recognize the difference between your personal purpose and your brand purpose because they aren't always the same.

Your personal purpose might be rooted in things like:

- Freedom and flexibility
- Creative expression
- Building a lifestyle that aligns with your values
- Earning income on your own terms

These internal motivations are powerful. They give you the courage to start something new and help you keep going even when things get tough.

But your brand purpose isn't about you but the people you serve. It's the external expression of your mission: why your business exists from your audience's perspective.

Here's one way to think about it:

- **Your personal purpose is the fuel:** it's what drives you forward.
- **Your brand purpose is the map:** it shows others where you're going and invites them to come along.

You need both. Your personal purpose gives your business soul. However, your brand purpose gives it focus and resonance in the market.

When your internal "why" connects directly to the impact you want to make for others, your business becomes something truly powerful when those two purposes align. Your messaging becomes clearer. Your decisions become easier. And your audience feels it. People can tell when a brand is rooted in something real.

In the upcoming exercise at the end of this chapter, you'll explore both angles: what drives you and how to translate that into a brand purpose that clearly and intentionally serves your audience.

A Word on Vision and Mission

You may have heard terms like vision and mission statements in your reading or during business planning. These concepts are closely related to purpose but serve slightly different functions.

- **Vision** is about the future. It's aspirational. It asks, "What do I want the world to look like if my business succeeds?"

- **Mission** is about action. It focuses on the present and answers, "What am I doing right now to make that vision real?"

- **Purpose** is the emotional and strategic through-line. It connects your mission to your values and audience. It's the anchor that keeps you aligned.

While you don't need separate statements for each of these (especially not in the early stages), thinking through them can help clarify what you're building and why it matters.

What If You're Still Figuring It Out?

Many small business owners feel unsure about their purpose, especially in the early stages. You might be offering services you're good at, or maybe you spotted a gap in the market and decided to fill it. Perhaps you're still narrowing your niche, clarifying your audience, or experimenting to see what actually sticks.

That's okay. It's normal.

Defining your brand purpose isn't about locking yourself into a narrow path forever. It's about choosing a direction that feels meaningful right now, something you care about enough to build around. You can always refine your purpose as your experience deepens and your clarity grows.

Your purpose doesn't have to be polished or poetic to be powerful. It doesn't have to be a tagline or a mission statement you print on your website tomorrow. It just needs to be honest.

Start with what you know:

- What kinds of people do you feel drawn to help?

- What problems have you solved that you'd want to help others navigate?

- What values do you want your business to reflect?

- What change would feel satisfying to contribute to, even in small ways?

Even something as simple as "I want to help people like me avoid the struggle I went through" is a valid and compelling starting point.

Your purpose can evolve, and it should. But the sooner you start making decisions based on what matters to you, the more aligned your business will feel and the easier it will be to attract clients or customers who connect with what you stand for.

So, if you're still figuring it out, that's not a reason to delay. It's an invitation to explore.

EXERCISE
Clarify Your Purpose

Your brand purpose is the "why" behind your business—but for many small business owners, it's closely tied to personal motivation, values, and lived experience.

The purpose of this exercise is to help you explore both your **personal why** and your **business purpose** and begin connecting the dots between the two.

Download this Exercise at TrembleDesign.com/BrandBooks
Use the space provided below to answer the questions, or grab the printable version of the exercise pages for additional flexibility.

Part 1: Your Personal Why

This section helps you reflect on the internal motivation behind your business. It's not about strategy—it's about you.

What inspired you to start your business or pursue this kind of work? *Think about your desire for freedom, creativity, service, or personal growth.*

_____

_____

_____

_____

_____

_____

What lights you up about the work you do?

What tasks or outcomes make you feel energized, proud, or deeply satisfied?

_____

_____

_____

_____

_____

_____

What kind of change do you want to create in the world, or someone's life? *This might be big-picture or very specific to your niche.*

_____

_____

_____

_____

_____

Who do you feel most called to help and why? *Describe the types of people or causes you feel personally connected to.*

_____

_____

_____

_____

_____

_____

_____

_____

Part 2: Your Brand Purpose

Now, shift your perspective outward. Your brand purpose is about why your business exists for other people. It's your personal why translated into service.

What led you to start this business?
Think back to that early spark. Was it a skill you wanted to use, a gap you noticed, or a problem you wanted to solve?

_____

_____

_____

_____

_____

_____

_____

What motivates you to keep going when things get hard?
What values or beliefs keep you committed, even on the tough days?

_____

_____

_____

_____

_____

_____

_____

What change are you creating for your clients, customers, or community? *How are people better off because they worked with you?*

_____

_____

_____

_____

_____

_____

_____

What do you want people to remember about your business? *What's the feeling, outcome, or impression you want to leave behind?*

_____

_____

_____

_____

_____

_____

_____

Crafting Your Purpose Statement

Once you've explored both your personal and brand purpose, try writing a short statement that captures the heart of your "why."

Example Purpose Statements:

- **Accounting Solopreneur:** I help independent professionals and small business owners take control of their finances so they can make smarter decisions and feel more confident about their future.

- **Small IT Cybersecurity Business**: We help growing companies protect their digital assets and reduce risk so they can focus on scaling their business without worrying about cybersecurity threats.

- **Nonprofit for Autism Education:** We help children with autism access personalized educational support so they can build essential skills and thrive in everyday life.

Use this sentence structure as a starting point:

I help [audience] to [achieve, feel, or overcome], so they can [benefit or result].

Start by filling in the blanks with what comes naturally, then play with the wording. Try multiple versions. Don't worry about making it perfect on the first try, this is a draft to help you get clarity. The more variations you explore, the easier it will be to spot the words or phrases that feel most true to you.

You might create a version that's straightforward and another that's more emotional or aspirational. Think of this as a brainstorming session, not a final exam.

I help _____

to _____

so they can _____

I help _____

to _____

so they can _____

I help _____

to _____

so they can _____

This is your brand purpose, the heartbeat of your brand. Let it evolve as needed, but make sure it always reflects what matters most to you and the people you serve.

CHAPTER 3
Brand Values

What Do You Stand For?

Every strong brand is built on a set of core values. These values act like a compass; they guide your decisions, shape your messaging, and influence the experience your audience has with you.

Whether you've taken the time to write them down or not, your values are already present in your business. They show up in how you treat clients, how you talk about your work, what kinds of opportunities you pursue, and what you say no to.

When I started building my business full time – transitioning from a secure job into self-employment – I thought I had a strong sense of what I stood for. Personally, I've always lived by a quiet code: honesty, curiosity, kindness, accountability. But when I sat down to define the values that would shape how I ran my business and served my clients, I realized I needed more clarity. It wasn't just about naming what mattered to me, I had to ask:

- Which values are central to how I want to run my business?

- Which values need to be visible to my clients and collaborators?

- Which values will resonate with the people I most want to serve?

I struggled at first to articulate these internal principles. But once I did, it changed everything. My brand felt more grounded, consistent, and me. I stopped questioning if I was "doing it right" and started making choices that felt aligned.

The exercise at the end of this chapter walks you through the exact process I used to define those values. Whether refining what you already know or starting from scratch, this chapter will help you bring those unspoken beliefs into the light, give them language, and ensure they're actively guiding your business, not just floating in the background.

Values Aren't Just Nice Words on a Wall

It's easy to think of brand values as something only large corporations care about – buzzwords like integrity, excellence, or innovation displayed in a company lobby or slapped onto an "About Us" page. But without context, those words often ring hollow.

For small business owners and solopreneurs, brand values carry a deeper, more personal meaning. They aren't just phrases that sound good; they're the quiet compass behind every decision you make. When you're the one wearing all the hats, values become the filter you use to choose what to build, how to show up, and who to work with.

Running a values-based business means your products, services, messaging, customer experience, and even your visual identity are all shaped through the lens of what you believe in. These values influence how you position yourself in the market and how others experience your brand.

When you define your brand values with intention, they:

- Help you stay consistent across platforms and client interactions

- Shape the tone and personality of your brand voice

- Create alignment between your business and your audience

- Guide decisions when things feel uncertain or messy

In short, your values keep your brand human, grounded, and trustworthy. They give your brand a sense of character, something people can recognize and connect with. And that connection matters. In the end, people are drawn to businesses that share their values. It's not just about what you do but what you stand for and how that comes through in everything you create.

What Do Brand Values Look Like in Real Life?

Let's look at some examples – not just of words, but of what they look like in action.

Imagine a brand that names "**Transparency**" as a core value. That might show up in how it writes pricing pages, communicates delays or mistakes, or talks openly about its process.

Or consider a brand built on "**Creativity**." Maybe it sells design work that challenges conventional thinking, experiments with new ideas, or brings playfulness into traditionally formal spaces.

Values aren't theoretical. They're practical. They show up in how you onboard new clients, how you handle feedback, the tone of your emails or website copy, the vendors or platforms you partner with, the types of clients you work with, or the causes you support.

When your values are clear and consistent, your brand feels more trustworthy because people sense that you stand for something. That consistency builds recognition, loyalty, and respect.

Aligning Personal and Brand Values

If you're a solopreneur or the founder of a small team, your personal values and your brand values are likely intertwined. That's a good thing because your beliefs are probably part of the reason your business exists.

But it's still worth pausing to ask: Are my personal values the same as my brand values? Should they be?

Sometimes, they're a direct match. For example, if you deeply value collaboration and your business offers collaborative consulting, that's easy alignment. Other times, your business may take on a slightly different voice than you personally would. For instance, you might be introverted, but your brand needs to be bolder or more authoritative to serve your audience well.

The key here is to recognize the difference and make intentional choices. When you define your brand values, you're not just identifying what you believe but determining what your business stands for and how those beliefs translate into action.

Choosing the Right Values

If brand purpose is the destination that drives your business forward, then values are the compass that keeps you aligned along the way.

Values aren't just surface-level buzzwords. When chosen with intention, they become the foundation for how you show up, serve others, and make decisions, even when no one's watching. They create continuity between what you believe, how you work, and how others experience your brand.

But many business owners make one of two common mistakes when defining their values:

- They choose vague, generic words that sound good but lack real meaning.

- They select a long list of words that ultimately dilute their focus and become hard to remember, let alone apply.

Three to five values are the sweet spot when choosing words to guide your business. This gives you enough range to capture the key principles that guide your work without becoming overwhelmed or inconsistent.

Your brand may feel one-dimensional or underdeveloped if you identify fewer than three values. But if you choose more than five, it becomes hard to consistently apply them, especially if you're a solo business owner trying to use them as decision-making tools.

This isn't about picking the most impressive words but choosing values that mean something to you. Values that are clear enough to guide you through hard choices, shape your messaging, and align you with the right clients. They should be words you can explain to someone else in a conversation, not just post on your website, but actually live out in your business.

The following exercise will lay the groundwork for building a value-based business that reflects who you are and resonates with the people you're here to serve.

Brand Values Brainstorm List

This is a long list of words with potential value and sparking ideas. Use this list as inspiration. Highlight the ones that resonate with you. Don't overthink it, just notice what feels true.

Once you've highlighted the words that resonate with you, move on to the Exercise in the next section.

Remember: there are no right or wrong answers here. Your values don't need to sound impressive or match anyone else's. They just need to feel meaningful to you. This process is about recognizing what matters most in how you run your business, how you serve your clients, and how you want to show up in the world. Clarity on your values will influence everything from your messaging to your client experience and serve as a powerful filter when facing tough decisions down the road.

I've categorized the values in the list below to keep them organized, but feel free to cross categories if there's a value that stands out to you.

- **Operational Values**: These guide how your business functions, makes decisions, and delivers services.

- **Relational Values:** These shape how you interact with clients, collaborators, and your community.

- **Creative + Visionary Values**: These reflect how you approach creativity, innovation, and long-term thinking.

- **Personal + Foundational Values**: These come from your personal worldview and define your deeper "why."

BRAND CORE VALUES IDEA LIST

Operational Values

Clarity	Craftsmanship	Structure	Improvement
Simplicity	Precision	Order	Innovation
Efficiency	Consistency	Timeliness	Resourcefulness
Excellence	Reliability	Discipline	Responsiveness
Quality	Accountability	Focus	Expertise
Mastery	Professionalism	Sustainability	Stewardship

Relational Values

Integrity	Empathy	Inclusion	Collaboration
Honesty	Listening	Diversity	Connection
Transparency	Trustworthiness	Patience	Service
Respect	Fairness	Encouragement	Community
Kindness	Generosity	Loyalty	Teamwork
Compassion	Equity	Support	Gratitude

Creative + Visionary Values

Creativity	Exploration	Growth	Courage
Curiosity	Imagination	Learning	Risk-taking
Originality	Boldness	Wisdom	Optimism
Beauty	Playfulness	Adventure	Passion
Inspiratio	Joy	Enthusiasm	Energy
Vision	Innovation	Flexibility	

Personal + Foundational Values

Purpose	Health	Humility	Responsibility
Freedom	Calm	Self-awareness	Confidence
Independence	Reflection	Intentionality	Authenticity
Autonomy	Mindfulness	Resilience	Honesty
Balance	Spirituality	Grit	Trust
Well-being	Faith	Forgiveness	Stability

EXERCISE
Core Values Discovery

In this exercise, you'll identify the values that guide your business. Because your personal and professional life are often closely intertwined, you'll likely end up with two related lists:

- A list of values that guide your **personal life**
- A set of core values that serve as a compass for **your brand**

As a solopreneur or small business owner, you are closer to the core of your business than a CEO of a large corporation might be. This exercise is uniquely designed to help you identify how your personal values and business values interlock or diverge. Let's walk through the process step-by-step.

> **Download this Exercise at TrembleDesign.com/BrandBooks**
> Use the space provided below to answer the questions, or grab the printable version of the exercise pages for additional flexibility.

Step 1: Start with Your Personal Values

Begin by naming the core beliefs and guiding principles that define who **you** are. These are the values that shape your life decisions, relationships, and everyday choices.

Use the list on the previous page as a starting point, if you need to. Write down the **three to five words** that represent your personal values, then describe what each one means to you.

You might start with a dictionary definition, but try to follow it with a sentence or two about how that value shows up in your life. What does it look like in action? Why does it matter to you?

My Personal Values

_____   _____

_____   _____

_____   _____

_____   _____

Step 2: Brainstorm Your Business Values

Now shift your focus to your business. Create a list of values that align with how you want to show up professionally. Don't overthink it. Write down as many words as come to mind without editing or filtering.

Values can be emotional (empathy), practical (efficiency), or philosophical (freedom, equity). Think about the goals you've set for your business, the kinds of people you serve, and the promises you want your brand to deliver.

Consider the following questions:

- What principles guide how I run my business?

- What do I value in the people I work with?

- What behaviors do I expect from myself or admire in others?

- What am I unwilling to compromise on?

My Business Values

_____   _____

_____   _____

_____   _____

_____   _____

Step 3: Group and Prioritize

Look through your list and begin grouping related values together. For example:

- *Transparency, Honesty, and Openness* are grouped together.
- *Excellence and Attention to detail* are grouped together.
- *Freedom and Autonomy* are grouped together.

Once grouped, a single word will likely emerge to describe that group of words. Narrow your brainstormed list to **three to five values** that most clearly reflect the heart of your brand. These are your core values; the values that should consistently guide your decisions and communication.

Groups or Similar Values

_____   _____

_____   _____

_____   _____

_____   _____

_____   _____

_____   _____

Use these questions to test your choices. If you can answer yes to each, you're on the right track.

- Would I make a difficult business decision based on this value?
- Does this value actually show up in the way I work and serve?
- Could someone outside the business recognize this value in my messaging or how I am positioned in the market?

Step 4: Define What The Values Look Like in Action

Now, bring your values to life by describing how they show up in your business. You'll write a sentence or two about each value and how that abstract idea shows up in real-world situations while running your business.

Here are a couple of examples:

- **Value: Clarity**
  In Action: We simplify complex ideas so our clients always know where they stand and what comes next. We avoid jargon and speak plainly.

- **Value: Respect**
  In Action: We listen fully, communicate directly, and treat every client and collaborator as a valued partner.

This step transforms abstract words into tangible behaviors. That's what makes values useful and powerful.

Value: _____

In Action: _____

_____

Value: _____

In Action: _____

_____

Value: _____

In Action: _____

_____

Value: _____

In Action: _____

_____

Value: _____

In Action: _____

_____

Value: _____

In Action: _____

_____

Wrapping Up

By the end of this exercise, you should be able to name and define your core brand values clearly. These values should feel real, recognizable, and deeply connected to how you want to run your business.

You'll start to see how these values shape your tone of voice in the next chapter and influence your brand positioning later in the book. They aren't just nice words to display; they're the roots of everything you're building.

CHAPTER 4
Brand Personality
How You Show Up

Your brand personality is how your business shows up visually, verbally, and emotionally. It's the combination of traits, tone, and energy that people experience when they interact with you.

This chapter will focus on one key part of that personality: your voice. Specifically, it will discuss how your business sounds in writing and how to make that voice feel clear, consistent, and unmistakably you.

We'll go deeper into personality and expression in Book 2: Brand Personality, but for now, this chapter will help you lay the groundwork. You'll start identifying the traits, tone, and patterns that shape how your brand communicates and connects.

There's a moment every business owner encounters: you sit down to write an About page, a social caption, a welcome email, and nothing sounds right. Too stiff? Too casual? Too vague? You know what you want to say, but the tone never seems to land.

That's a brand voice problem. And you're not alone.

Your brand voice is one of the most powerful and often overlooked tools in your brand strategy. It's the tone, language, and rhythm you use in emails, blog posts, website copy, social media, and more. When shaped with intention, your voice becomes one of your brand's most recognizable and memorable parts.

This chapter will help you clarify and use that voice consistently across your business. But first, let's define what "voice" means in a brand context.

What Is Brand Voice?

Your brand voice is the **personality behind your words**. It's how your business "speaks" to the world, whether in a blog post, client proposal, Instagram caption, or customer support message.

It's not *just* what you say, it's how you say it.

For example, two businesses offering the same service could sound completely different. A bookkeeping firm might choose a calm, professional voice that builds trust through clarity and precision. Another might lean into humor and casual language to make finances feel approachable for creative entrepreneurs.

Neither approach is wrong. Your brand voice should reflect:

- Your core values and how those values show up in your business
- Your audience's needs and expectations
- The tone you want your business to be remembered for

Your voice is the verbal expression of your brand's personality, and it's just as important as your purpose, values, positioning, and visual identity.

Voice vs. Tone: What's the Difference?

As you begin defining how your brand communicates, you'll hear the terms voice and tone come up often. They're closely related, but they aren't interchangeable and understanding the difference between them will help you write and speak more consistently across every part of your business.

Your **brand voice** is the steady, recognizable personality behind your words. It reflects your values, style, and emotional presence; it makes your communication feel like you every time someone interacts with your brand.

Your **tone**, on the other hand, is how you adapt that voice to different situations. It reflects the emotional context of the message and how you sound when you're welcoming someone new, responding to a complaint, or celebrating a milestone.

If your brand were a person, its **voice** would be its personality. Tone would be how they speak in a given moment, depending on the conversation.

For example, your brand voice might always be clear and encouraging, but your tone might shift to match the context:

- Friendly and informal in a social post
- Warm and celebratory in a client welcome message
- Calm and empathetic in a refund email

When your voice is clearly defined, adjusting your tone becomes much easier. You stay consistent but never robotic, and that flexibility is what makes your brand feel both human and reliable.

BRAND ARCHETYPES
Discovering Your Brand's Character

Just like people, brands have personalities, and those personalities influence how we show up, how we speak, and how people connect with us. One of the most useful tools for understanding your brand's personality is the concept of **brand archetypes**.

Brand archetypes are rooted in psychology and storytelling. They represent universal characters or roles that appear repeatedly in culture, literature, and advertising. When used thoughtfully, archetypes can help clarify your brand's emotional tone, guide your voice and visuals, and create a stronger connection with your audience.

You don't have to guess who your brand is "supposed" to be. Chances are, your brand already expresses some of these traits; you just haven't named them yet. And once you do, everything else becomes easier: tone of voice, messaging style, brand photography, even how you name your offers or write a welcome email.

Archetypes can also help you differentiate yourself in a crowded market. If every brand in your niche speaks with the same authoritative "expert" tone, and your brand naturally feels more like a guide, caregiver, or creator, leaning into that difference becomes a powerful asset.

Most brands reflect one dominant archetype and possibly a secondary archetype. Even if you've never heard of them before, you've definitely seen them in action:

- A brand with a **Caregiver** archetype (Dove or the Red Cross) might sound nurturing, warm, and reassuring. It's focused on protecting, supporting, and creating a sense of safety and trust.

- An **Explorer** brand (Jeep or National Geographic) might sound adventurous, curious, and open to discovery. It might be focused on helping others push boundaries and find their own path.

- A **Sage** brand (TED or Harvard Business Review) might sound confident, insightful, and polished. It is focused on sharing knowledge, delivering clarity, and helping others make informed decisions.

You don't have to pick just one, but identifying one or two archetypes that align with your values (and, later, your audience) can help you refine your voice and tone. Are you the approachable guide? The bold innovator? The calm caregiver? The trusted advisor?

The following pages contain a list of common brand archetypes. Use them to explore the personality your brand already expresses or the one you want to adopt more intentionally.

THE 12 BRAND ARCHETYPES | *At a Glance*

The Innocent – Optimistic, honest, and pure. This brand sees the world through a hopeful lens and seeks to inspire simplicity, happiness, or goodness. Examples: Dove, Coca-Cola, Aveeno

The Everyman (or Regular Guy/Gal) – Relatable, approachable, and grounded. These brands make people feel seen and included, no frills, no pretense. Examples: IKEA, Target, Budweiser

The Hero – Driven, confident, and determined to make the world better. This brand helps people rise to a challenge or reach their full potential. Examples: Nike, FedEx, Gatorade

The Outlaw (or Rebel) – Bold, disruptive, and unapologetic. This brand rejects the status quo and calls its audience to question the rules. Examples: Harley-Davidson, Diesel, Ben & Jerry's

The Explorer – Adventurous, curious, and independent. Explorer brands invite their audience to seek new experiences or forge their own path. Examples: Jeep, REI, National Geographic

The Creator – Imaginative, expressive, and visionary. These brands help people build, design, or dream, turning ideas into reality. Examples: Adobe, Lego, Crayola

The Ruler – Authoritative, polished, and in control. This brand conveys leadership, order, and expertise, often with a premium or professional edge. Examples: Mercedes-Benz, Rolex, American Express

The Magician – Transformative, insightful, and inspiring. These brands create change by helping people see new possibilities or unlock hidden potential. Examples: Disney, Apple, TED

The Lover – Passionate, sensory, and emotionally driven. This brand centers on connection, beauty, and indulgence—often in lifestyle or luxury spaces. Examples: Chanel, Godiva, Victoria's Secret

The Caregiver – Compassionate, nurturing, and protective. Caregiver brands make people feel safe, supported, and valued. Examples: The Red Cross, Johnson & Johnson, TOMS

The Jester – Playful, witty, and entertaining. These brands use humor and joy to create connections and stand out in memorable ways. Examples: Old Spice, M&M's, Mailchimp

The Sage – Wise, thoughtful, and analytical. Sage brands seek to educate, inform, and guide their audience with clarity and truth. Examples: Harvard, Google, The New York Times

> *We'll cover Brand Archetypes in much more detail in Book 2 of the Brand Building for Small Business series:* **Brand Personality - Create meaningful connection through identity, voice, and messaging**

Why Voice Matters for Small Business Owners

As a solopreneur or small business owner, you're likely writing most of your copy yourself, at least for now. That means you're making dozens of micro-decisions about language, tone, and message every week. Without a clear voice, those decisions can quickly become overwhelming. But when your voice is clear and intentional:

- You stop second-guessing yourself, and writing becomes easier, faster, and more intuitive.

- You sound more consistent across platforms. Everything from proposals to social media will sound like you.

- You build trust faster because people feel like they hear from the same person every time.

And if you ever decide to hire help, whether a copywriter, social media manager, or virtual assistant, your defined voice becomes a guide they can follow from day one.

Where Your Brand Voice Shows Up

Whether you've defined it or not, your brand voice is already at work. It's woven into every word your business puts into the world, sometimes intentionally, sometimes by default.

Your voice shows up everywhere your brand communicates, on your website and homepage, in your email newsletters and sales funnels, across social media captions, replies, and DMs. It's present in your client welcome kits, proposals, onboarding documents, and in the way you describe your products, services, and pricing. Even your automated messages, out-of-office replies, and voicemail contribute to your brand voice.

Anywhere your brand speaks, whether digitally or in person, your voice is part of the experience.

Even if your brand is quiet or understated, your voice still shapes how people experience you. The question isn't if you have a voice, it's whether you're using it intentionally.

When your voice is clear and consistent, your brand becomes easier to recognize and trust. People know what to expect. They feel like they know you, even if you've never met. That kind of connection leads to loyalty, and it starts by making your voice a conscious choice rather than a byproduct of habit.

How to Find Your Brand Voice

The good news? You're not starting from scratch. If you've worked through the earlier chapters of this book, you've already identified your **purpose** and **core values**. Those are two of the biggest ingredients in your brand voice.

In later chapters, you'll define your **audience** and your **positioning**, further shaping how your voice comes across in real-world interactions.

Here are a few examples of how your brand strategy informs your voice:

- If one of your core values is transparency, your voice might be direct, honest, and open, even when delivering complex information.

- If your purpose is to empower overwhelmed people, your voice might be calm, clear, and reassuring.

- If your audience is made up of busy, ambitious professionals, your voice might need to sound confident, concise, and results-oriented.

Your brand voice should be a natural extension of what you believe and how you serve. It's not about sounding clever or trendy, it's about sounding like you, consistently, across every platform.

Your brand voice isn't just how you speak; it's how you connect. Connection builds trust, loyalty, and long-term relationships. That's the true power of voice: not just saying the right words but saying them in a way that makes people feel seen, heard, and supported.

People notice when your brand sounds like you, the values-based, intentional business owner you are. And more importantly, they remember.

EXERCISE
Define Your Brand Voice

Brand Tone Spectrum

Your brand voice reflects your personality and values, but also needs to resonate with your audience. Use the chart below to explore where your brand voice falls on a spectrum of traits.

> *Download this Exercise at TrembleDesign.com/BrandBooks*
> *Use the space provided below to answer the questions, or grab the printable version of the exercise pages for additional flexibility.*

There are no right or wrong answers; **just place a dot along the line** where it feels most natural, authentic, and aligned with how you want your brand to show up in the world.

Fun _____ Serious

Casual _____ Formal

Relaxed _____ Professional

Modern _____ Traditional

Vibrant _____ Muted

Unique _____ Familiar

Youthful _____ Mature

Playful _____ Authoritative

Conversational _____ Polished

Inspiring _____ Practical

Once you've mapped your tone, we'll build on it with descriptive voice attributes to round out your brand's personality.

Brand Voice Descriptors

Now that you've explored your brand voice across tone spectrums, let's take it further. Review the list of descriptive voice traits on the next page and choose 3–5 words that best capture how you want your brand to sound. These descriptors will help guide your writing style, tone, and messaging across every part of your business, from your website and emails to your proposals and social media.

Highlight the words that stand out to you, or write in your own if something better fits. Remember: the goal isn't to sound like everyone else; it's to sound like you.

Clarity & Confidence	Connection & Warmth	Creativity & Style
Clear	Warm	Witty
Concise	Empathetic	Quirky
Confident	Friendly	Clever
Assertive	Encouraging	Playful
Direct	Supportive	Artistic
No-nonsense	Honest	Expressive
Instructive	Open	Bold
Transparent	Welcoming	Experimental
	Personal	Imaginative

Expertise & Authority	Inspire & Motivate	My Voice Descriptors
Professional	Uplifting	•
Knowledgeable	Passionate	
Thoughtful	Purpose-driven	•
Analytical	Visionary	•
Smart	Ambitious	•
Credible	Empowering	•
Researched	Hopeful	
Strategic	Energizing	•
Sophisticated		

Your brand voice might blend a few of these traits! Try picking 3–5 words that most align with how you want your brand to sound and feel, then test them in your copy to see what feels right.

Write a One-Sentence Summary

Use this template to bring your tone and voice descriptors together. Craft a sentence you can refer to whenever you write content for your business. (We'll cover your audience in the next chapter, so feel free to come back to this exercise after you complete that chapter.)

Template:
"My brand voice is *[descriptor]*, *[descriptor]*, and *[descriptor]*. It sounds like *[brand archetype]* talking to *[audience]* in a way that feels *[emotion/experience]*."

Example:
My brand voice is calm, confident, and clear. It sounds like a trusted guide talking to an overwhelmed founder in a way that feels empowering and non-judgmental.

Write a One-Sentence Summary of Your Brand

_____

_____

_____

_____

_____

_____

_____

_____

Step 3: Put It Into Practice

Take your chosen descriptors and try writing 2–3 short brand messages that reflect your voice. Here are a few prompts to get you started:

- A social media welcome message for new followers
- An email response to a missed client meeting
- A homepage intro sentence: "Welcome. I help _____ so they can _____."

As you write, ask yourself: Does this sound like the version of myself I want to bring into my brand?

You don't have to get it perfect today, but by naming your voice and practicing it, you'll begin to write more easily, confidently, and consistently.

CHAPTER 5
Your Audience

Who Are You For?

When you're running a small business, it's easy to fall into the habit of trying to be everything to everyone. You might offer a wide range of services, appeal to multiple industries, or shape your messaging based on what you think people want to hear.

> *If you try to speak to everyone,*
> *you end up connecting with no one.*

When your audience is too broad, you spend all your time and energy trying to appeal to too many people. Your message becomes diluted, your offers feel scattered, and your brand lacks the clarity to truly resonate. The people you're trying to talk to don't recognize themselves in your message, so they ignore you.

That's why defining your audience is one of the most important steps in building a strong brand. And when I say "define" your audience, I mean that you need to know your audience intimately and be prepared to connect with them on a personal level. It's not about excluding people. It's about clearly understanding who your business is best suited to help and how you can show up for those people authentically and impactfully.

This chapter will help you get focused, specific, and strategic about who you serve and how to connect with them.

Why Audience Clarity Matters

When you know who you're speaking to, you stop guessing and start truly connecting. Clarity about your audience gives your brand direction. It shapes your tone, informs your message, and influences how you build your offers. It helps you show up in a relevant way, not just be visible.

When you begin to understand your audience, more specifically, your ideal customer, you'll need to know the answers to some basic questions:

- What problem are they trying to solve?
- How do they typically search for answers?
- What tone, language, or approach will resonate with them emotionally and intellectually?

Your job is to position yourself in their path, so your brand already feels like the right fit when they search for a solution. When you can articulate their struggle, sometimes even better than they can, you create an instant bond. You're no longer just another service provider or product on the shelf. You become someone who gets it.

Most marketing strategies are built on the philosophy that people buy from companies they "know, like, and trust." And when you can speak clearly to your potential customers about the problems they are trying to solve, you instantly become the type of brand they want to buy from.

That sense of being seen and understood is powerful. It builds trust before the first sale, before the first conversation. It's what helps potential clients go from curious to committed.

Audience clarity also prevents wasted effort. Stop trying to speak to "everyone" and focus your energy on where it matters most. Your content will become more focused, your offers will become more aligned, and your marketing will become more efficient. And that clarity ripples outward into every part of your brand:

- Your voice sounds more natural
- Your messaging becomes easier to write
- Your visual identity feels more aligned
- Your confidence grows because you know exactly who you're talking to and how you can help them.

The first step is to define your ideal audience with specificity and care so your brand can connect, serve, and grow from a place of genuine alignment. That clarity doesn't just make things easier; it makes your brand more focused, trustworthy, and effective.

Here are just a few ways audience clarity shapes your brand:

- **It sharpens your messaging** – When you understand how your audience talks about their problems, you can speak in their language, not industry jargon or generic promises. You can reflect their goals, fears, and frustrations to make them feel seen.

- **It helps you design better offers** – When you know what your audience truly needs and what they've already tried, you can craft relevant, timely, and results-driven offers. You're not guessing; you're responding with intention.

- **It makes your voice more personal and direct** – You're not broadcasting into the void or writing for a vague demographic. You know exactly who you're talking to, so your tone feels more natural, trustworthy, and human.

- **It shows you where to show up** – When you know where your audience spends their time–online and offline–you can position your brand where they're already looking. Whether that's SEO keywords, in-person events, podcasts, or social platforms, you can stop chasing trends and start meeting your audience where they are.

- **It gives you confidence** – When you know who you serve and how you help, you can say no to distractions. You stop trying to be everything to everyone and start showing up for the people who are most likely to benefit from what you offer.

Defining Your "Right-Fit" People

There's a lot of talk in marketing circles about "ideal clients" or "target markets," but here's the angle I want you to take: **think about right-fit relationships.**

- Who are the people you want to work with?

- Who gets the most value from what you offer?

- Who energizes you, aligns with your values, and needs what you're naturally great at?

This approach works whether you're a service provider, a nonprofit, a coach, or a product-based business owner. The goal isn't to shrink your audience; it's to sharpen your focus so you can speak more clearly, show up more intentionally, and attract the people who are most likely to say, "Yes, this is exactly what I've been looking for."

But defining your audience is only half the work. You must also ensure that your brand aligns with what that audience is seeking. It's not just about identifying the right people; it's about becoming the kind of brand that feels like a natural fit for their needs, goals, and values.

When your brand communicates in a way that mirrors your audience's mindset, language, and priorities, you don't have to work as hard to get their attention. They'll recognize themselves in your message. They'll feel seen. They'll trust you faster.

So, yes, get specific about who you serve. But also ask yourself if you are showing up in a way that resonates with the people I want to reach. Does my voice, offer, and brand experience align with the solution they're already searching for?

You might already have a solid idea of your ideal customer, especially if you've worked with a few of them already. Or you might still be figuring it out. Either way, you're in the right place.

The exercise at the end of this chapter will help you clarify that picture so you can speak more directly, serve more intentionally, and start attracting the people your business is truly built to help.

Go Beyond Demographics

Many traditional marketing exercises begin with basic demographic information: age, gender, income, education level, and location. While that data has its place, especially in larger campaigns or ad targeting, it rarely tells the full story, especially for small businesses built on trust, relationships, and values.

If you've worked with a range of clients or customers already, you have access to something far more useful: **real-world insight** into the people you enjoy serving, and who benefit most from your work. Start by looking back at past clients or customers and asking:

- Who did I love working with and why?

- What made the work feel easy, energizing, or rewarding?

- What did they need from me? What problem were they trying to solve?

- How did they find me or hear about my business?

- Were there any early signs that we were a great fit?

And just as important, look closely at past clients that would not fit your ideal audience profile. Ask yourself:

- Which of my past clients felt like a mismatch?

- What made the work harder than it needed to be?

- Were there mismatched expectations, communication gaps, or conflicting values?

These reflections give you powerful clues about what to look for and what to avoid. Pay attention to patterns. What did your best-fit clients value? What traits or behaviors made the work go smoothly? What goals or personalities mesh naturally with your approach?

Demographics alone won't reveal this. But **psychographics, behaviors, shared values, and emotional drivers** will. As you clarify your ideal audience, ask deeper questions:

- What do they need emotionally, functionally, practically?
- What challenges do they have, and how are they trying to solve them?
- What do they care deeply about? (*Efficiency? Beauty? Simplicity?*)
- What kind of language do they use to describe their problems?
- What emotions drive their decisions? (*Fear? Hope? Overwhelm?*)
- Where do they go to look for solutions? (*Search engines? Forums? Word of mouth?*)

This is how real connection begins. When you understand your audience at this level, your brand becomes more than just visible, it becomes recognizable. And when the right people feel seen, understood, and supported, they're far more likely to trust you and choose you.

Know Who You're Not For

Audience clarity isn't just about attraction; it's also about discernment. It's one thing to know who you want to work with. Knowing who you don't want to attract is just as important. Not every client or customer will be a great fit, and that's okay.

Defining what "not a fit" looks like helps you to spot red flags earlier, set clear boundaries, and protect your time, energy, and reputation.

Think back to a client or project that didn't go well. Maybe it drained you, felt misaligned from the start, or left you questioning your process. You don't need to dwell on the negative, but you can learn from it. Ask yourself:

- What made that client or project a poor fit?

- Were there warning signs you ignored?

- What values or communication styles clashed?

- How did that experience affect your motivation or confidence?

- What would you do differently next time?

You might even create a "Red Flag Avatar," a semi-fictional profile that helps you recognize patterns of misalignment before you say yes. Give it a name if it helps. Keep it in mind when reviewing inquiries or vetting opportunities. This isn't about judging people. It's about protecting your alignment.

Because clarity in both directions. Understanding who's right for you and who's not makes your business stronger, your messaging clearer, and your decision-making easier.

Audience Is a Two-Way Relationship

Many business owners overlook the simple truth that you get to choose your audience, too. Yes, market research matters. Yes, it's essential to understand who needs what you offer. But your brand isn't just built around what they want; it should also reflect who you want to work with.

Who do you understand best? Who do you enjoy serving? What types of clients or customers light you up?

You may have left a corporate job and realized you feel most fulfilled working with nonprofits. Maybe you've had difficult experiences with certain industries or working styles and want to avoid those moving forward. That's not you being picky. Okay, yes, it's you being picky. But you're being picky for the right reasons, protecting your business and your energy.

You are not obligated to serve everyone who shows up.

You're not serving the masses. You're offering your services or products to one real, imperfect human who needs what you offer. The better you understand that person and clearly define who's not a fit, the easier it becomes to build a business rooted in alignment.

The more clear you are about who you're speaking to – and who you're not – the more you'll attract people who are the right fit, and gently repel those who aren't. You don't need everyone to choose you. You need the right ones to recognize that you're exactly what they've been looking for.

The more specific you are about who your ideal audience is and the more clearly you speak their language when describing the solution you offer, the easier it becomes for the right people to recognize themselves in your brand. When they do, they're far more likely to say, "Yes. This is exactly what I've been looking for."

EXERCISE
Define Your Right-Fit Audience

Now that you've reflected on your past clients, clarified your values, and explored what truly matters to your business, it's time to turn those insights into something tangible: **your Ideal Audience Avatar.**

This isn't about building a fictional sales persona. It's about articulating the real traits, goals, and emotional drivers of the people your business is best suited to help—so you can speak to them with confidence, clarity, and care.

> *Download this Exercise at TrembleDesign.com/BrandBooks*
> *Use the space provided below to answer the questions, or grab the printable version of the exercise pages for additional flexibility.*

Step 1: Define Your Ideal Audience Avatar

Start by giving your avatar a name. (Yes, really!) Thinking of them as a specific person, rather than a vague group, will help you create more focused messaging and more aligned offers.

Use the prompts below to describe them in detail:

- Start with the demographics (age, gender, location, income level)
- What do they do? (Profession, role, or life stage)
- What are they trying to achieve or change?
- What challenges or obstacles are they facing?
- What have they already tried, or what's holding them back?
- What do they value? (Speed? Simplicity? Excellence? Integrity?)
- What kind of support are they looking for?

- What words do they use to describe their struggles?

- What emotions are driving their decisions? (Frustration? Fear? Ambition? Hope? Overwhelm?)

- Where do they go when looking for help? (Google, referrals, forums, in-person events)

Next, describe what changes after working with you or buying your products:

- What do they walk away with emotionally and practically?

- How do they feel after their problem is solved?

- What does success look like through their eyes?

Use the space on the following page to begin building your Ideal Audience Avatar.

Remember, if you offer several different types of services or products, you may also have several different Audience Avatars. Simply repeat this process for each audience segment that you serve.

Audience Demographics

Demographics	**Avatar Name**	
	Gender	
	Age	
	Location	
	Income	
	Education	
	Family Status	
	Profession	
	Job Role	
	Life Stage	

Audience Challenges and Your Solution

Challenge & Solution	Challenge/Obstacle	
	Solutions tried	
	Support they need	
	What they value	
	Keywords for Challenge/Obstable	
	Emotions	
	Where are they looking for help?	
After Purchase	What will they get?	
	How do they feel?	
	What does success look like to them?	

Now that you've identified the key characteristics about your ideal audience avatar and their challenges, write a paragraph (or two) that brings this person to life. Give them a name and use AI to generate a photograph of this fictitious person. This additional layer of "humanizing" your ideal audience avatar will make it easier to write content, design offers, or review client leads.

_____

_____

_____

_____

_____

_____

_____

_____

_____

_____

_____

_____

_____

_____

_____

_____

_____

Step 2: Identify Red Flags

Clarity goes both ways. Knowing who isn't a fit is just as valuable as knowing who is. Think about a past client or project that drained your energy or didn't align with your values. What traits, behaviors, or red flags showed up?

Use these prompts to guide your reflection:

- What made that person or project a poor fit?
- Were there early warning signs you missed?
- What expectations, values, or communication styles didn't align and did they effect the outcome of the project?
- What would you do differently next time?

You should create a short Red Flag Avatar to represent this mismatch. If it helps, give them a name and keep them in mind when qualifying leads or setting boundaries.

Use the process you just completed to create your Red Flag Avatar.

_____

_____

_____

_____

_____

_____

_____

_____

_____

CHAPTER 6
Brand Positioning

What Makes You Different?

"Positioning" is one of those business terms that can feel vague or overly corporate, like something meant for Fortune 500 brands, ad agencies, or tech startups pitching to investors. But the truth is, every brand has a position, whether you've defined it or not.

Will you choose your position intentionally, or will you let the market choose it for you?

Brand positioning is the space you occupy in the mind of your ideal customer. It's the mental snapshot people carry about your business—the impression you leave, the value you're known for, and the reason someone chooses you over a competitor with similar offerings.

| *Reputation + Relevance = Brand Position*

Your reputation reflects the experience you create. Your relevance reflects how closely your work aligns with what your audience needs. Together, they define how you're perceived and how clearly you stand apart.

Positioning isn't about dominating your niche or shouting louder than everyone else. It's about making it obvious to the right people that your approach, process, personality, and values make you the best choice for them. It's less about broad competition and more about strategic alignment.

In that sense, positioning is the bridge between the internal strategy you've been building (your purpose, values, voice, and audience) and how your brand shows up in the world. When those pieces align, your brand becomes easier to recognize and choose.

Positioning for Small Businesses

You can stand out without shouting or disrupting the market. You don't need to invent a revolutionary product or completely redefine your industry to stand out. Most small businesses, especially service-based ones, differentiate through subtle but meaningful distinctions. Instead of chasing trends or "market domination," they focus on clarity, alignment, and trust.

Here are a few powerful ways small brands position themselves:

- **Your audience focus:** You serve a specific kind of person with specific needs, not the masses.

- **Your process**: You use a framework, philosophy, or delivery method that reflects your unique approach.

- **Your personality**: Your communication feels human, consistent, and grounded in your brand's voice.

- **Your perspective**: You bring a point of view that offers clarity or challenges the status quo.

- **Your values**: You lead with principles your audience recognizes and respects, such as equity, sustainability, or accessibility.

None of these elements need to be loud or flashy. But when they come together intentionally, they shape how your audience experiences your brand and whether they trust you enough to choose you.

Positioning is all about owning your space in the minds and hearts of the people you're here to serve.

Positioning as a Solopreneur or Small Team

If you're a solo business owner or leading a small, founder-led team, your positioning often overlaps with your personal story, values, and lived experience. That's not a liability. It's a strength. Embrace your position and leverage the unique benefits you can offer your customers.

You're not just selling a product or delivering a service. You're building relationships, making decisions in real time, and infusing your work with purpose. Larger companies often wish they could replicate that level of human connection.

As a solopreneur, your positioning might include:

- A **niche audience** you understand deeply, because you've been there yourself, or you're still part of that audience

- A **delivery style** that reflects your personal strengths or way of working

- A **story or journey** that resonates with the people you want to help

- A **tone and presence** that feels clear, reassuring, hopeful, empowering, or bold

- A set of **non-negotiable values** that shape how you operate, who you serve, and what you say no to

Your positioning is not about perfection, it's about resonance. You don't need a slick brand or a big platform to stand out. You just need to show up with clarity and intention, and consistently communicate what makes you the right choice for your right-fit audience.

Brand Positioning Examples

Before you define your own position, it can be helpful to see how other brands do it, especially when their approach feels clear, consistent, and well-aligned with their audience.

These examples aren't meant to be copied, but studied. Each one reflects a distinct audience, voice, and value proposition that reinforces the brand's identity and builds trust. As you read through them, notice what makes each brand stand out and how you might apply similar clarity to your own positioning.

Kit – Email Tools for Creators

- **Positioning:** An email-first platform built for creators who want to grow their business and own their audience.

  Formerly ConvertKit, Kit rebranded to reflect its expanded mission: serving creators with tools beyond email. Its features, voice, and product design all reinforce one message: This is built for you. With automation, creator networking, and a growing app ecosystem, Kit helps creators grow on their own terms.

- **Why it works**: Kit focuses on a clearly defined audience and aligns every part of the brand with their needs.

Warby Parker – Stylish Eyewear Without the Markup

- **Positioning:** Affordable, fashionable glasses for people who value design, transparency, and social good.

  Warby Parker disrupted the eyewear market with a direct-to-consumer model, simple pricing, and a give-back program. Their voice is bright, modern, and accessible, just like their customer experience.

- **Why it works**: Warby Parker leads with values and clarity, making it easy for customers to say yes.

Jeep Wrangler – Built for Adventure

- **Positioning:** The go-anywhere vehicle for people who crave freedom and exploration.

  Jeep doesn't try to be sleek or luxurious; it leans hard into its identity as rugged, off-road-ready, and unshakably adventurous. From its taglines to its visuals, everything says "freedom." And it's not just marketing. Jeep has built a loyal community of drivers who wave at each other on the road and bond over a shared love of the journey.

- **Why it works:** Jeep knows exactly who it's for and makes sure that the audience feels seen.

Aaron Draplin – Big Personality, Blue-Collar Design

- **Positioning**: Authentic, hard-working design for real people, with no pretense.

  Aaron Draplin has built a fiercely loyal following by being unmistakably himself. His brand is rooted in practicality, storytelling, and a love of working-class grit. From bold, utilitarian logos to co-founding Field Notes, everything Draplin touches feels intentional and proudly analog. He's not polished or corporate; he leans into his personality and voice to attract clients and fans.

- **Why it works**: His brand feels like a handshake, not a pitch. That kind of grounded clarity attracts clients who want the real deal.

The Positioning Statement

Now that you understand positioning and why it matters, let's focus on a simple framework to help you articulate your brand's place in the market. A strong positioning statement clarifies what you offer, who it's for, and what makes it different without sounding like a sales pitch.

You don't need a long or complicated explanation. Just a few clear, intentional sentences can give your brand a sharper edge in the minds of your audience. Here's a classic structure to work from:

I help _____ *[specific audience]* _____

achieve_____ *[specific result]* _____

through _____ *[your unique approach or offering]* _____ .

This isn't a tagline or a slogan, it's a strategic tool that brings direction and focus to your brand. You might use pieces of it in your messaging, but its primary purpose is to keep you (and your team) aligned as you write marketing copy, craft service descriptions, respond to inquiries, or decide what to build next.

The core components define as:

- **Who** your brand, service, or product is for

- **What** result or transformation is your audience seeking

- **How** you deliver that result in a way that feels distinct and aligned with your brand

This clarity gives your audience a reason to choose you, and it gives you a filter for what to say yes to as your brand and business evolve.

It's All About Authenticity

Brand positioning isn't about being the biggest, loudest, or most impressive name in your niche. It's about being the **right fit** for the people who need you most.

When you can clearly explain who you serve, what you help them achieve, and why your approach is different, your brand stops sounding generic and starts sounding trustworthy.

That's the power of positioning. It helps people self-select, builds confidence before the first conversation, and sets the tone for relationships built on alignment, not just transaction.

Because at the end of the day, the goal isn't to serve everyone. It's to serve the people who will get the most value from what you offer. And when your brand reflects that clearly and consistently, you don't have to convince anyone, you simply connect.

That's what authentic positioning does. It helps the right people recognize that you're exactly what they've been looking for.

Want to Go Deeper on Brand Positioning?

This chapter has given you a starting point, but there's much more to explore. Book 3 in the *Brand Building for Small Business* is your next step. *Brand Position: Own Your Niche and Be Remembered* will walk you through refining your niche, articulating your brand's promise, and building a position that sets you apart in a crowded market, without sacrificing your values or personality.

Visit TrembleDesign.com/BrandBooks to be alerted about future book releases.

EXERCISE
Write Your Positioning Statement

Use the following prompts to guide your thinking. If you've completed the earlier exercises in previous chapters, you already have most of the raw material. Now it's time to bring it together.

> *Download this Exercise at TrembleDesign.com/BrandBooks*
> *Use the space provided below to answer the questions, or grab the printable version of the exercise pages for additional flexibility.*

Step 1: Identify the Core Components

Who is your ideal audience?
Be specific – not just "small business owners" but something as specific as "women-owned consulting businesses in their first five years."

_____

_____

_____

_____

_____

What is the key outcome or benefit you help them achieve?
This might be financial (more revenue), emotional (more clarity), or operational (less overwhelm).

_____

_____

_____

_____

What makes your process or approach unique?
This could be your style, your values, your background, or a method you use.

_____

_____

_____

_____

_____

Step 2: Write a First Draft

Use the template we discussed in the last section to craft the first draft of your Brand Positioning Statement. Don't worry about perfection, just aim for clarity and truth. You may wish to write several versions to share with team members, partners, or trusted advisors for feedback and refinement.

I help _____ *[specific audience]* _____

achieve_____ *[specific result]* _____

through _____ *[your unique approach or offering]* _____.

Try writing several drafts to test

I help _____

achieve _____

through _____

I help _____

achieve _____

through _____

I help _____

achieve _____

through _____

I help _____

achieve _____

through _____

I help _____

achieve _____

through _____

I help _____

achieve _____

through _____

I help _____

achieve _____

through _____

These don't need to be perfect or public-facing; they're just tools to help you stay grounded in what you do, who it's for, and why it matters.

Need inspiration? Here are a few examples of brand positioning statements and why they work.

Small Brick-and-Mortar Business (e.g., Take-Out Restaurant)

> *We help busy families eat well during the week by offering fresh, affordable take-home meals, prepared daily in our neighborhood kitchen.*

Why it works: Clearly defines the audience (busy families), the result (healthy weekday meals), and the delivery method (locally prepared, take-home meals). It feels rooted in community but purposeful.

Solopreneur Professional Service (e.g., Accountant)

> *I help small business owners simplify their finances and make smarter decisions through straightforward bookkeeping and hands-on financial guidance.*

Why it works: It emphasizes both the emotional and practical outcome (clarity + smarter decisions), paired with a clear, personal delivery approach. There is no fluff, just value and service.

Service-Based Business with a Small Team (e.g., Consultant)

> *We help mission-driven nonprofits clarify their messaging and design compelling campaigns that drive real impact, without the overwhelm.*

Why it works: Focuses on a specific audience (nonprofits), a clear result (clarity + campaign success), and positions the team as a supportive, strategic partner.

Step 3: Gut Check

Once you've drafted your statement, you'll want to share it with key members of your team, trusted advisors, or collaborators to get their honest feedback. Some questions you can ask yourself include:

- Does this feel like me and the brand I've started building?

- Would my ideal audience recognize themselves in this?

- Is the outcome meaningful and specific enough to be compelling?

- Can I deliver what I'm promising?

- What feedback have I gotten from team members, partners, or trusted advisors?

You'll likely refine your statement as your brand evolves or you develop new products or services. But even a working draft will help you stay focused and communicate more effectively.

Use the space here to capture feedback from collaborators and advisors and answers to the questions above.

_____

_____

_____

_____

_____

_____

_____

_____

PART 2

FROM STRATEGY TO ACTION

Align & Apply

You've built a thoughtful brand foundation, clarified your purpose, values, audience, voice, and positioning. You've put words to things that may have previously been fuzzy or intuitive, and you've created a strategic framework to guide every part of your business going forward.

Now it's time to bring that strategy to life.

In Part 2, you'll start by organizing what you've built into a clear, usable brand strategy document. Then you'll learn how to apply that strategy across your business, keep your brand aligned as things evolve, and make smart decisions as your business grows or shifts direction.

You don't need to have it all figured out. But you do need a system that helps you stay consistent, confident, and clear even as your business changes. Let's make sure the brand you've defined on paper becomes something you can actually use every day.

CHAPTER 7
Bringing It All Together

Branding can sometimes feel abstract. Words like "strategy," "alignment," and "positioning" sound great – but at the end of the day, you're probably asking: What do I actually do with all of this?

This chapter is where you start turning insights into action. You've done the deep work of defining what your brand stands for, who it's built to serve, and how it should sound and show up.

Now, it's time to step back, examine everything you've created, from purpose to personality, and evaluate it as a cohesive system. We'll take these workbook exercises and turn them into the operating system for your business.

Brand Strategy isn't just a collection of ideas on paper. It's a detailed blueprint you use to guide decisions, sharpen communication, and create consistency across every part of your business.

Before you move forward, it's time to zoom out and look at the big picture. Gather everything you've created in this workbook so far: your brand purpose, values, audience avatar, voice descriptors, positioning statement, and key brand traits.

> *Pause. Read through it all.*
> *Don't just skim, but really read it.*

Take a moment to reflect on what feels true, what might be missing, and what no longer fits. This is your opportunity to adjust anything that's evolved, add insights you've uncovered, or remove pieces that no longer align.

Your brand will continue to evolve over time, but for this next step, you need a working draft that reflects where you are right now and supports the direction you're heading. As you do your review, ask yourself:

- Is there a clear throughline? Do all the pieces feel like they belong to the same brand?

- Are there any contradictions? (Example: Your brand voice is bold, but your messaging feels generic.)

- Where do you feel strongest, and where are you still unclear?

- Are the traits and promises you want to be known for showing up in every part of your business?

Think of this as a brand alignment check. Your goal is to create internal consistency, a strategy that holds together on paper and actively supports everything your business does. And if something feels off or incomplete, that's not a failure; it's insight. Go back to the chapter that needs more attention. Redo the exercise. Add what's missing. This is your foundation and is worth refining until it feels solid.

Your Strategy Guides Everything

When your brand strategy is clear, it becomes a filter for every decision you make. It's the internal foundation you return to again and again, whether you're launching something new or refining what already exists.

Here are just a few of the decisions you might make on any given day and how your brand strategy helps guide them with clarity and consistency:

- **Messaging:**
  Does this website headline sound like you? Does this social post speak to the actual problem your audience is trying to solve, or is it just filling space? Whether you're writing an Instagram caption or drafting an email campaign, your voice and values should shape what you say and how you say it.

- **Visuals:**
  Do your brand colors, fonts, and photography reflect the personality and energy you want your brand to express? Does this billboard, flyer, or social graphic feel aligned with your audience's preferences, or will it feel off-brand and out of place?

- **Product Development:**
  Does this new product or service meet your audience's real needs, or is it just something you want to offer? Is it solving the right problem at the right time in a way that reflects your approach and values?

- **Client Experience:**
  From onboarding emails to intake forms to your refund policy, does how you handle clients reflect the tone, care, and clarity on which your brand is built? Are you reinforcing trust or creating friction that feels out of sync with your brand personality?

- **Collaboration:**
  Do your vendors, contractors, or creative partners understand the kind of brand you're building? Can they reinforce your strategy through their work, or do you need to better communicate your voice, standards, and expectations to get aligned?

When your strategy is unclear, these decisions can feel heavy, scattered, or disconnected. But when your brand strategy is solid and acts as the foundation of your business, everything starts to click. You stop reinventing the wheel whenever you launch a new offer or write a social post because you're building from the same clear, aligned core.

Your Brand Strategy Document

The exercise at the end of this chapter will walk you through the process of creating your Brand Strategy document. Thankfully, you don't need a 20-page brand manual. But you do need a concise, usable document that captures the essence of what you've built so far.

This becomes your go-to reference for every decision related to marketing, messaging, offers, or design. It also lays the foundation for your visual identity, so when it's time to design (or redesign) your logo, choose brand colors, or develop a cohesive look and feel, this document makes the process much easier, whether you're doing it yourself or working with a designer.

Your strategy document should include the most essential elements of your brand: your purpose, values, audience insights, voice and tone guidelines, and positioning statement.

If you've already begun defining your visual identity, like color palettes or typography, you can include those, too. The goal is to create a focused summary of who you are, what you stand for, and how your brand should show up in the world.

Remember, this isn't a one-and-done assignment. Your strategy document is a living resource. It should evolve as your business grows, your audience shifts, or your offers change. That's the beauty of having it in writing: it gives you something to revisit, refine, and rely on as you move forward with more clarity and confidence.

Strategy First, Style Guide Later

Your brand strategy document is not the same as a brand style guide, though eventually, the two will work together as a unified system.

The strategy document captures the why and how of your brand: your purpose, values, voice, audience, and positioning. It's the internal compass that guides everything your business says and does.

A brand style guide, on the other hand, focuses on visual execution. It includes specific guidelines for your logo, color palette, typography, imagery, and visual styling for things like graphics, photos, and video.

If you decide to hire a professional designer, your strategy document becomes an invaluable resource. It gives your designer everything they need to create a style guide that accurately reflects your brand, so your visuals are aligned with your message from the start.

You don't need a polished visual system yet, but the work you've done here will give you a head start when the time comes.

What Alignment Feels Like

You'll start to notice when your brand is aligned, internally and externally. Things feel smoother. You speak about your business with more clarity. You get more of the "right fit" inquiries. Your content gets easier to write. You trust yourself more because your decisions are rooted in something deeper than trends or guesswork.

That's the magic of a values-based brand. It doesn't shout to be heard, it simply resonates.

EXERCISE
Brand Strategy Summary Sheet

You've done the hard part. You've explored your purpose, clarified your values, defined your audience, found your voice, and claimed your position in the market. That's no small feat; most business owners never take the time to do this foundational work.

Now, it's time to bring it all together.

Use this page to compile the essential elements of your brand strategy into a clear, easy-to-reference summary. This will become your go-to document; something you return to repeatedly as you grow, communicate, and confidently make decisions.

As you complete each section, start with a single-sentence summary. Then expand on that summary with a few sentences about what it means and how you'll apply it in your business.

> *Download this Exercise at TrembleDesign.com/BrandBooks*
> *Use the space provided below to answer the questions, or grab the printable version of the exercise pages for additional flexibility.*

Brand Purpose

One-Sentence Summary:
Why does your business exist beyond making money?

_____

_____

_____

_____

_____

Application Prompt:
What does this purpose mean to you personally, and how will it show up in your client experience, messaging, or offers?

_____

_____

_____

_____

Audience Avatar *(Brief Description)*

One-Sentence Summary:
Who are you here to serve, and what do they need most?

_____

_____

_____

Application Prompt:
How will knowing this person shape how you show up, speak, and create solutions for them?

_____

_____

_____

_____

Brand Values

One-Sentence Summary:
What core principles guide how you run your business?

_____

_____

_____

_____

Application Prompt:
What do these values look like in action? How will they influence your boundaries, decisions, or client relationships?

_____

_____

_____

_____

Voice Descriptors

One-Sentence Summary:
What 3–5 words describe how your brand sounds when it communicates?

_____

_____

_____

_____

Application Prompt:
How will you carry that tone across your website, emails, social media, and conversations? What will you say "no" to in order to stay consistent?

_____

_____

_____

_____

Positioning Statement

One-Sentence Summary:
What makes you the right choice for your ideal audience?

_____

_____

_____

_____

Application Prompt:
What makes your approach unique or valuable, and how will you communicate that clearly in your brand messaging?

_____

_____

_____

_____

Now Start Using It

Once completed, keep this summary somewhere visible. Print the pages, tape them above your desk, share the summary with collaborators, and use it whenever you write, design, market, or plan.

Brand Alignment Checklist

Use this checklist to evaluate whether your brand's outward expression matches your defined strategy. For each item below, ask: Does this reflect my purpose, values, voice, audience, and positioning?

BRAND ALIGNMENT CHECKLIST

Messaging & Voice

- ❏ My brand voice is consistent across platforms (email, social, website, proposals, etc).

- ❏ My core values are reflected in how I communicate, not just what I say

- ❏ My messaging clearly states who I help, how I help, and what makes my approach different

- ❏ My words build trust and resonate with the audience I want to attract

- ❏ My tone and word choice reflect the brand personality I've defined

Positioning & Audience Fit

- ❏ I can clearly explain why someone should choose my business over another

- ❏ My website or marketing materials speak directly to the audience I most want to reach

- ❏ I highlight my unique process, philosophy, or value proposition

- ❏ My offers are tailored to the needs, language, and goals of my ideal customer

- ❏ I've made intentional choices about how I want my brand to be perceived in the market

Visual Identity

- ❏ My logo, colors, and fonts reflect the tone and personality I want to communicate.

- ❏ My visual style feels appropriate and appealing to my ideal audience

- ❏ My website, social media, and printed materials feel cohesive and recognizable

- ❏ My imagery (graphics, icons, photos, video) supports the message I want to convey

- ❏ My brand design choices reflect the positioning I want to occupy (e.g., bold vs. traditional, luxurious vs. accessible)

Final Check-In:

- ❏ Does my brand feel cohesive across every touchpoint?

- ❏ Would someone new to my business understand who I serve and how I help, within seconds?

CHAPTER 8
Audit, Evolve, and Grow

You've done deep, strategic work to clarify what your business stands for and how it should show up in the world. You've defined your purpose, values, audience, voice, and positioning. You've crafted a brand strategy that feels aligned, intentional, and rooted in what matters most to you and the people you serve.

You may have picked up this book because you already had a brand, but something wasn't working. Maybe your messaging felt vague, your visuals felt dated, or your offers no longer reflected the direction of your business.

That's where a brand audit comes in.

As mentioned in the last chapter, your brand is not a one-time project. It's a living system, an evolving reflection of how your business grows, adapts, and shows up in the world. And as you evolve, your brand needs room to evolve with you.

This chapter will help you:

- **Audit** your existing brand for alignment

- **Evolve** what's no longer working with clarity and purpose

- **Grow** with a strategy that supports your next phase of business

Whether starting fresh or refining what already exists, your brand strategy should become a tool you return to, not just a project you check off. Implementing your brand strategy becomes a habit system you build until it becomes muscle memory about how to apply it to every aspect of your business. Let's look at how to put that into practice.

Build Habits Around Your Brand

Your brand works best when used consistently, not just at launch, but every day. To build a more aligned, intuitive brand experience, create habits that support your strategy:

- **Create a brand reference sheet**
  Summarize your purpose, audience, values, voice, and positioning in one place. Use it whenever you write, design, or make decisions.

- **Schedule regular brand check-ins**
  Review your brand strategy every quarter. Ask: What's still aligned? What's shifted? What new insights do I need to integrate?

- **Use your voice guidelines consistently**
  If your brand sounds clear and confident on your website, don't sound vague or overly casual in your emails or posts. Keep your tone true across every platform.

- **Train collaborators and contractors**
  Whether you hire a copywriter, designer, or assistant, share your strategy with them. This will help them create work that strengthens, not dilutes, your brand.

Audit: Keep Your Brand in Check

Even the most thoughtful strategy can drift over time. Maybe you've evolved your services, started attracting a different type of client, or developed a sharper vision for where your business is headed. That's normal. As your business grows, your brand must grow with it.

But here's the challenge: when your day-to-day operations move fast, it's easy for your visuals, messaging, or client experience to fall out of sync with who you are now. That's why it's so important to build in regular brand check-ins.

A **brand audit** gives you the chance to evaluate what's still aligned, what feels outdated, and what needs attention. It's not about tearing everything down; it's about making sure the brand you show to the world matches the business you're actually running.

Here's how to approach an intentional, manageable brand audit:

- **Audit your brand assets**
  Look closely at your website, social media profiles, proposals, onboarding materials, and visual identity. Do these assets reflect my current voice, values, and purpose? Is my message still clear and positioned for the right people? Am I attracting the kind of clients I truly want to work with?

  This kind of honest review can help you spot what's still working and what may be due for a refresh.

- **Decide what to keep, tweak, or retire**
  Some pieces may only need minor adjustments (like updating a headline or refreshing a few photos), while others may require deeper work. Prioritize high-impact areas like your homepage, brand bio, or most-used client materials.

- **Make a plan, not a panic**
  You don't have to overhaul everything overnight. Set a realistic timeline for changes and create small milestone goals to track your progress. It's okay if the changes take three to six months to complete; just work on them gradually. Give yourself permission to evolve without burning it all down.

- **Roll out changes intentionally**
  Start with subtle, high-visibility touchpoints. Update your social bio, refine your elevator pitch, and refresh your intro emails. Let your brand strategy guide each step, and check in regularly as you grow.

Auditing your brand isn't a dramatic reset. It's a quiet recalibration; a way to ensure your strategy and expression stay in sync as you continue building something that reflects who you are and how you want to serve. Make this a habit, and your brand will always feel like a steady foundation, not something you have to second-guess.

> **Need more in-depth help with a brand audit?**
>
> If you found this section helpful, you'll love Book 4 in this *Brand Building for Small Business* book series: *Brand Audit – From Confusion to Clarity for Strategic Growth*. It walks you through a full brand audit process so you can confidently evaluate what's working, what's not, and what needs to evolve. Learn more at TrembleDesign.com/BrandBooks.
>
> If you'd prefer personalized support, I offer **1:1 Brand Audit Sessions** designed to give you clear, actionable feedback based on your unique business. Whether you need quick insights or a deeper review, I'd love to help. Learn more at TrembleDesign.com/brand-audit.

Evolve: Make a Plan to Realign

Sometimes, a brand needs more than a touch-up; it needs a shift.

Brand evolution happens when something significant changes in your business. It's not just a matter of tightening your message or refreshing a few visuals. It's a deeper realignment that responds to a new direction, a changing audience, or a shift in what your business offers.

Here are a few common signals that your brand may be ready to evolve:

- **You've introduced new products or services** that no longer fit your original brand's tone, visuals, or messaging.

- **Your leadership or ownership has changed**, and the new vision or values aren't fully reflected in your current brand.

- **Your audience has shifted**, demographics, expectations, or behaviors have changed, and you're no longer resonating the way you once did.

- **Customer feedback** highlights gaps, confusion, or dissatisfaction that point to a misalignment between your brand and your actual customer experience.

- **The competitive landscape has evolved,** and your positioning is no longer as clear or distinct as it once was.

- **You've outgrown your original identity**, what once felt modern and fresh, now feels outdated, overly narrow, or unrepresentative of who you've become.

Brand evolution doesn't mean scrapping everything you've built. It means revisiting the foundational elements of your brand—your purpose, values, audience, voice, and positioning—and updating them to reflect your current reality and future direction.

How to Navigate Brand Evolution

- **Revisit Your Strategy. Don't Guess**
  Start by reviewing each part of your brand strategy. What's still true? What needs to shift? Refine your purpose, audience, values, voice, and positioning in light of your business's new direction.

- **Engage Your Team (If You Have One)**
  If you have collaborators, employees, long-time partners, or your trusted circle of advisors, bring them into the process early. Their insight, especially from client-facing roles, can uncover blind spots and reinforce clarity across the business.

- **Clarify What You're Keeping vs. Changing**
  A brand evolution doesn't have to mean a full rebrand. Maybe your logo still works, but your messaging needs a shift. Maybe

your audience has changed, but your values haven't. Outline what stays the same and what will change.

- **Update Your External Touchpoints Strategically**
  Begin applying your evolved brand to your website, service pages, content strategy, onboarding process, and visuals. Start with high-impact or high-traffic areas where your audience will feel the difference most.

- **Communicate the Shift**
  Whether it's a quiet internal shift or a more public reintroduction, make sure your audience understands what's changed and why. Use this as a moment to reestablish trust and show the intentionality behind the evolution.

Brand evolution is not a failure of your past brand; it's a reflection of your growth. Businesses change, markets shift, and people evolve. A strong brand evolves with them. And when it's done well, your brand doesn't just keep up; it leads.

Grow: When Your Brand Needs to Scale With You

When your business grows, your brand has to grow with it.

You may have started as a solopreneur and now lead a small team, or even a full-blown agency. Maybe you've gone viral, added new product lines, or seen a sharp increase in visibility and sales. Growth is exciting, but it also reveals cracks in your original brand strategy, especially if that strategy was built for a much smaller version of your business.

A brand strategy that worked beautifully when it was just you and a few loyal clients may no longer be enough to guide a team, maintain consistency across platforms, or support your expanded audience.

Here are some signs that your brand is struggling to keep up with growth:

- You've grown a team, but they're unsure how to write, design, or speak in your brand voice

- Your visuals or messaging no longer match the level of professionalism or polish your audience expects

- You're attracting a wider audience, but your brand still feels tailored to your original niche

- Your internal documents and onboarding materials are inconsistent or nonexistent

- Your offers have scaled, but your positioning hasn't kept pace

- You're being recognized more publicly, but your brand seems designed for a quieter, more private version of your business.

How to Scale Your Brand Strategy Alongside Your Business

When your business grows quickly, it's easy for your brand to get left behind. But for growth to be sustainable, your brand needs to evolve alongside your business, matching its pace, scale, and visibility. The strategies below will help you stay aligned as you expand.

- **Revisit Your Strategy With Scale in Mind**
  Go back to the foundational elements—purpose, values, audience, voice, and positioning—and ask: Does this still reflect who we are and where we're going? You may need to expand or clarify certain sections to better support a broader audience or a larger team.

- **Document Everything**
  What was once intuitive now needs to be shared. Create a living brand guide that includes messaging samples, tone of voice guidelines, audience snapshots, and visual direction.

  Document your processes and establish SOP (standard operating procedures) so your team runs efficiently and knows how to get help when working on projects that affect the brand. This will become your internal training tool and protect your brand as you delegate more outward-facing work.

- **Bring Your Team Along**
  Your team can't follow what hasn't been clearly defined. Share your strategy and guide, and host a brand alignment meeting. Make sure everyone understands not just what the brand is, but why it exists, and how their role connects to it.

- **Prioritize Consistency at Scale**
  As your business grows, consistency becomes harder, but more essential. Set brand standards for client experience, onboarding, social media, and internal communications. Empower your team to use your brand voice confidently and consistently.

- **Assess Your Tools and Platforms**
  Does your website still reflect your brand's scale and sophistication? Do your content systems support a growing team? Your infrastructure and brand should evolve with your operational needs as they grow, not lag behind them.

Growth is a gift, but it's also a test. When your brand strategy can stretch to meet your business's size, visibility, and complexity, you not only grow but grow with clarity. And that's what turns momentum into long-term success.

When to Get Outside Help

You've already done more strategic brand work than most small business owners ever will. That alone is something to be proud of. But even with a strong foundation, you don't have to implement it all alone.

At some point, you might feel ready to bring in professional support, whether that's a designer to develop your visual identity, a copywriter to bring your voice to life, or a strategist to help fine-tune and implement your next steps. When that time comes, your brand strategy becomes an incredible asset. It gives any collaborator, designer, writer, or creative partner instant insight into who you are, what you stand for, and how to create work that aligns with your business. You'll know it's time when:

- You're stuck on how to move from strategy to execution

- You're second-guessing your visuals or messaging

- You want an outside perspective to sharpen what you've already created

- You need a clear, professional brand guide to use with your team or contractors

And if you're already feeling that hesitation or overwhelm, I can help. Whether you need a **focused 1:1 Brand Clarity Session**, a half-day strategy workshop, or help translating your strategy into visual and verbal expression, I'd love to help.

Visit TrembleDesign.com to explore brand clarity sessions and next-step services. You don't have to do everything alone anymore. You've already built something intentional. Now it's time to bring it to life, on your terms, with the right help when needed.

You're the Brand Steward Now

You don't need a huge team, a perfect logo, or a clever tagline to build a meaningful brand. You just need clarity, consistency, and the courage to show up with intention.

You've laid a strong foundation. You've done the deep work. Now it's time to trust yourself and use your strategy to shape the kind of business that feels like you.

Whether you continue refining it solo or bring in expert support, your brand now has direction, depth, and purpose. That's the real power of strategy.

Continue Your Branding Journey

The Brand Building Workbook Series

Building a brand is more than just choosing a logo or picking your favorite colors; it's about creating the emotional fingerprint of your business. It's how people recognize you, remember you, and connect with the deeper purpose behind what you do.

When your brand is rooted in strategy and aligned with your values, it becomes the foundation for every decision you make—from your messaging and visuals to your offers and partnerships. A strong brand isn't built overnight, but with intention and clarity, it becomes one of your greatest business assets.

This book is just the beginning.

If you're a small business owner building something intentional from the ground up, you deserve resources that respect your time, values, and vision. That's exactly why I created the Brand Building for Small Business series, a collection of short, highly-focused and practical workbooks designed to help you build a brand that feels aligned, authentic, and truly your own.

Each workbook explores a different aspect of branding, with the same practical tools, thoughtful guidance, and approachable tone you've experienced here. These books are created specifically for solo and small business owners who care deeply about doing things right, without wasting time, chasing trends, or cutting corners.

In this book, we've briefly touched on brand personality, positioning, and audits. The remaining workbooks in the series allow you to dive deeper into each area to continue refining and strengthening your brand with clarity and intention.

These workbooks are made for solo and small business owners who care deeply about doing things right, without wasting time, chasing trends, or cutting corners.

Book 2: Brand Personality – Create Meaningful Connection Through Identity, Voice, and Messaging

Your business already has a personality, whether you've defined it or not. This book helps you shape your brand's character traits, emotional fingerprint, voice, tone, and style.

Book 3: Brand Positioning – Own Your Niche and Be Remembered

Clarify your unique place in the market so the right people remember and choose you. This book walks you through strategically positioning your brand and standing out without shouting.

Book 4: Brand Audit – From Confusion to Clarity for Strategic Growth

If your brand feels inconsistent or outdated, this guide will help you assess what's working, what's not, and how to refresh your brand without starting from scratch.

Want to be the first to know when new books launch?

Visit TrembleDesign.com/BrandBooks to sign up for launch updates, access bonus resources, and get alerts when the next books in the *Brand Building for Small Business* series are released.

Let's build something great one intentional step at a time.

APPENDIX
Glossary of Brand Terms

Audience – The group of people your business is built to serve. A well-defined audience helps you focus your message, tailor your offers, and build stronger relationships. Your ideal audience isn't just about demographics; it's about shared needs, values, and the specific problems your work is designed to solve.

Brand – The reputation and emotional connection people have with your business. Your brand is how others experience you through your messaging, visuals, tone, and interactions. It's not just what you say but what people remember and feel when they engage with your business.

Brand Alignment – The harmony between your internal brand strategy (purpose, values, voice, positioning) and your external brand expression (visuals, messaging, client experience). When your brand is aligned, it builds trust, clarity, and consistency across every touchpoint.

Branding – Branding is the intentional process of shaping how your business is perceived. It includes how your brand looks (visual identity), sounds (voice and messaging), and feels (client experience and emotional tone). Branding brings your strategy to life through creative and practical execution.

Brand Identity – The combined visual and verbal system that brings your brand to life. This includes your logo, color palette, typography, tone of voice, and messaging guidelines. Your brand identity translates your strategy into design and communication elements people can see and hear.

Brand Positioning – The space your business occupies in your audience's mind, and what makes you different from others in your field. It's not just about being the "best" or the "first," but the right fit for the right people. Positioning connects your offer, values, and message with your audience's concerns.

Brand Personality – The set of human traits and characteristics that define how your brand looks, sounds, and feels. It shapes your business's emotional impression and influences how people relate to it. Your brand personality helps guide your voice, tone, visuals, and overall brand experience, making your business feel more consistent, memorable, and relatable.

Brand Purpose – Your purpose is the deeper reason your business exists beyond making money. It reflects what you stand for, why you do what you do, and how you want to make an impact. Your purpose brings meaning to your work and builds emotional resonance with your audience. Your mission explains what you do, but your purpose explains why it matters.

Brand Strategy – The internal roadmap for how your brand communicates, connects, and shows up in the world. It includes your purpose, values, voice, audience, and positioning, and guides your decisions about messaging, visuals, offers, and marketing. A strong brand strategy brings clarity to everything you create.

Brand Values – The consistent style, tone, and language your brand uses across all platforms. It's the verbal personality of your brand and helps create familiarity, trust, and recognition. A strong brand voice reflects your values and personality and guides how you communicate in everything from websites to emails to social media.

Brand Voice – The verbal personality of your brand. You use consistent style, tone, and word choice to communicate across all platforms. Your voice helps your brand feel familiar and trustworthy, whether writing emails, sharing on social media, or delivering client updates.

Customer Journey – The full experience someone has with your brand, from first discovering you to becoming a loyal customer (and beyond). It includes every stage of interaction, including awareness, interest, decision-making, purchase, and retention. A clear brand strategy helps you create a consistent, meaningful experience at every step.

Ideal Client / Audience Avatar – A semi-fictional profile of your perfect-fit client or customer, based on real insights and goals. This tool helps humanize your messaging and speak directly to the people who will benefit most from your work. A strong avatar goes beyond demographics and includes values, needs, motivations, behaviors, and decision-making cues.

Marketing – The tools, platforms, and strategies you use to promote your business and connect with your audience. Marketing is how you share your brand's message, while branding is the foundation that gives that message meaning and direction.

Mission Statement – A statement that defines what your business does, who it serves, and how it delivers its work. It's more action-oriented than your purpose and often appears in external-facing materials like websites or proposals. Your mission explains what you do. Your purpose explains why it matters.

Positioning Statement – A sentence that summarizes who you help, what you help them achieve, and how you uniquely deliver that outcome. It distills your brand's focus and how it fits into a clear message that can guide internal decisions and external communication.

Tone – The emotional inflection of your brand voice. While your voice stays consistent, your tone may shift depending on the context or message such as being encouraging, calm, enthusiastic, formal, etc. Tone helps you stay human and responsive while maintaining brand integrity.

Touchpoint – Any moment of contact between your brand and your audience. This could include your website, emails, social media posts, client onboarding, packaging, voicemail greeting, or even word-of-mouth.

Visual Identity – The visual expression of your brand, including your logo, color palette, typography, imagery, and design style. These elements work together to create a cohesive visual experience and clearly communicate your brand personality.

About the Author

Pam Tremble is a brand strategist, creative director, and long-time solopreneur who believes that thoughtful strategy and clear design can transform how small businesses show up in the world. With a background in graphic design, marketing, and creative leadership, Pam brings more than two decades of experience in helping purpose-driven businesses and nonprofits clarify their message and express their brand with confidence.

Through her business, **Tremble Design Studio**, she supports clients with strategic brand planning, logo design, brand identity development, and brand audits. She often serves as the creative partner behind the scenes for teams that want to focus more on impact and less on overwhelm.

Pam believes in the power of DIY learning, values-first leadership, and intentional stewardship of your brand, even (and especially) if you're a business of one. She created this workbook to help fellow solopreneurs and small business owners develop a brand they can grow into without losing themselves in the process.

When she's not designing or coaching, you'll likely find her crocheting prayer shawls and lapghans for those in need, fighting for desk space against the demands of a needy cat, writing her next book, nerding out about stationery, or working on side quests from her home in Michigan.

Learn more or connect with Pam at TrembleDesign.com.

www.ingramcontent.com/pod-product-compliance
Lightning Source LLC
Chambersburg PA
CBHW071430210326
41597CB00020B/3736